Study Guide to A
Elmes, Kantowitz, a

Research Methods in Psychology

Sixth Edition

Joseph B. Thompson

Washington and Lee University

Brooks/Cole Publishing Company

I(T)P® An International Thomson Publishing Company

Pacific Grove • Albany • Belmont • Bonn • Boston • Cincinnati • Detroit
Johannesburg • London • Madrid • Melbourne • Mexico City
New York • Paris • Singapore • Tokyo • Toronto • Washington

Senior Assistant Editor: *Faith B. Stoddard*
Editorial Assistant: *Stephanie M. Andersen*
Marketing Team: *Alicia Barelli, Christine Davis, Aaron Eden*
Production Editor: *Laurel Jackson*
Cover Design: *Roy R. Neuhaus*
Printing and Binding: *Webcom Limited*

For more information, contact:

BROOKS/COLE PUBLISHING COMPANY
511 Forest Lodge Road
Pacific Grove, CA 93950
USA

International Thomson Editores
Seneca 53
Col. Polanco
11560 México, D. F., México

International Thomson Publishing Europe
Berkshire House 168-173
High Holborn
London WC1V 7AA
England

International Thomson Publishing Japan
Hirakawacho Kyowa Building, 3F
2-2-1 Hirakawacho
Chiyoda-ku, Tokyo 102
Japan

Thomas Nelson Australia
102 Dodds Street
South Melbourne, 3205
Victoria, Australia

International Thomson Publishing Asia
221 Henderson Road
#05-10 Henderson Building
Singapore 0315

Nelson Canada
1120 Birchmount Road
Scarborough, Ontario
Canada M1K 5G4

International Thomson Publishing GmbH
Königswinterer Strasse 418
53227 Bonn
Germany

Printed in Canada

5   4   3   2

ISBN 0-534-35813-6

Table of Contents

CHAPTER 1
Beginning Psychological Research

SUMMARY
I.   Why do psychological research?
      A.   To understand why humans and animals behave as they do.
            1.   Behavior generally refers to directly observable actions.
            2.   Covert processes may be inferred from observable behavior.
      B.   Research is driven by
            1.   Theories and hypotheses (basic research).
            2.   Practical real-world problems (applied research).
II.   Why study research?
      A.   To learn how to conduct sound research yourself.
      B.   To learn to evaluate the research of others.
            1.   **Critical thinking** can provide an informed judgment of the value of research
III. In a good experiment:
      A.   Some aspect of behavior (the **dependent variable**) is observed while
      B.   Some aspect of the environment (the **independent variable**) is manipulated and
      C.   Other possible influences of behavior (**control variables**) are held constant
            1.   **Confounding** occurs when an unintended variable changes together with the independent variable, thus invalidating the experimental results.
IV.   Getting started on research
      A.   Get an idea from
            1.   Observing the world with a critical eye,
            2.   Talking with experts, and
            3.   Reading journal articles.

    B.   Develop a **testable hypothesis** that
        1.   States the relationship between two variables, and
        2.   Specifies how these variables are to be measured.
    C.   Review relevant journal articles to
        1.   Determine what is already known about your hypothesis, and help
        2.   Refine your research plan.
    D.   Conduct **pilot research** to
        1.   Refine your research procedures, and
        2.   To see if you have selected appropriate levels of the independent variable.

V.   Pitfalls in research include:
    A.   Ethical concerns
        1.   Be sure to treat your humans subjects as you would wish to be treated.
        2.   Treat your animal subjects humanely.
    B.   Biases
        1.   **Inadvertent researcher bias** (or expectations) can influence the results of your research. Attempts to control this kind of bias include
            a.   Strict use of a **protocol**, to ensure that subjects are treated uniformly, and
        2.   Use of a blind or a **double-blind design** in which either the subject, or both the subject and the researcher do not know which treatment the subject has received.
    C.   A common pitfall in animal research is **anthropomorphism**, attributing human characteristics such as emotions, feelings, and thoughts to lower animals.
    D.   Ambiguous communication of research results.
        1.   **Operational definitions**, which state how measurements of a variable are made, are commonly used to achieve reliable communication between scientists.

VI.   Concluding the research project entails
    A.   Collecting the data,
    B.   Statistically analyzing the data,
    C.   Interpreting the results, and
    D.   Writing-up the study

.Key Term Matching

1.

___ anthropomorphizing

___ confounding

___ inadvertent researcher bias

    a. allowing a uncontrolled variable to change together with changes in the independent variable

    b. attributing human characteristics to lower animals

    c. expectations of the data collector influence the research outcome

2.

___ control variable

___ dependent variable

___ independent variable

    a. potential influence on the dependent variable that is held constant

    b. what the experimenter manipulates

    c. what the experimenter measures

3.

___ double-blind design

___ operational definition

___ pilot research

___ treating animals humanely

    a. a control for researcher bias

    b. a way to reduce ambiguous communication

    c. means of dealing with an ethical issue

    d. useful in identifying useful levels of the independent variable

4.

___ critical thinker

___ placebo

___ *PsychInfo*

___ *Psychological Abstracts*

___ Stroop Effect

___ testable hypothesis

    a. makes informed or reasoned judgments

    b. computerized search engine for psychological literature

    c. pharmacologically inert substance

    d. slowing of the naming of the number of objects when the objects are digits

    e. statement of the relationship between two measurable variables

    f. collection of brief abstracts of psychological research papers

PROGRAMMED REVIEW

1. _____ refers to overt activities of people and animals.

2. Psychologists conduct research for two basic reasons: to develop theoretical _____ of a behavior of interest, and to solve _____

    _____.

3. A _____ is a person who makes an informed or reasoned judgment about the value of something.

4. In an experiment, the _____ _____ is deliberately manipulated to determine its effect on behavior.

5. The _____ _____ is the aspect of behavior that is measured in a psychological experiment.

6. _____ _____ are held constant so that they will not inadvertently influence the behavior of interest in an experiment.

7. _____ occurs when a variable not of interest happens to change together with changes in the independent variable.

8. Science begins with _____ - both as a source of data and as a source for research ideas.

9. Professors and other _____ may suggest research projects, or help you refine your own research ideas.

10. The _____ _____ is a good general resource that will help you find journal articles relevant to your research ideas.

11. After you have identified a problem or idea to investigate, the next step is to formulate a _____ _____.

12. Hypotheses will not be testable unless they include variables that are both _____ and _____.

13. In addition to suggesting ideas, a _____ _____ will help you discover what is already known about your hypothesis.

14. Another name for preliminary research is _____ research.

EXPERIMENTAL PROJECT

One of the best ways to learn what it takes to conduct a research project is to actually design and carry out your own research. However, you can get a good idea of the problems associated with conducting research by going through the research process up to the point of actually collecting data. Presented below are two possible research ideas. Select one of these ideas and then attempt to design a research project to address one (or more) of the issues raised by this problem. Be sure to formulate a testable hypothesis, perform at least a brief review of the relevant literature and determine if pilot research is necessary. Finally, design a project that would be feasible to conduct given the resources available to you.

Problem 1. A number of memory improvement books (e.g. Higbee, 1977) state that mental imagery helps people to remember. What type of evidence could we obtain that might help us determine how valid this claim is?

Problem 2. One of your friends claims that football players are better athletes than gymnasts or swimmers. Is there any evidence to support this claim? What type of research would be needed to address this issue?

REFERENCE

Higbee, K. L.(1977). *Your Memory: How it Works and How to Improve it.* Englewood Cliffs, N.J.: Prentice Hall.

EXPERIMENTAL DILEMMA

A counseling psychologist believes that physical exercise will help patients suffering from chronic depression. The psychologist is currently treating 39 people who are suffering from chronic depression. Thirty-six of these people said that they would be willing to participate in an experiment if the experiment might help them and might also provide information that would help the psychologist to learn more about how to help depressed people.

The psychologist administered a standard paper and pencil test to measure how depressed his subjects were before treatment. The psychologist used these scores to match 12 groups of three people who scored about the same on the depression test. These three people were then randomly assigned to treatment conditions.

People in condition 1 were then asked to engage in some sort of outdoors exercise three times a week, people in condition 2 exercised five times a week, and people in condition 3 were not asked to exercise, but they were asked to spend some time outdoors at least three times a week.

At the end of the six week experiment the subjects took another paper and pencil depression test. The results showed that all subjects were now rated as less depressed than they were at the beginning of the experiment. However, the subjects in conditions 1 and 2 had improved more than the subjects in condition 3. Subjects in conditions 1 and 2 had improved the same amount over the six week period.

The psychologist concluded that exercise provides help above and beyond that provided by simply spending time outdoors. He also concluded that three days of exercise a week was enough to benefit the depressed person.

What was the hypothesis tested by the researcher? What were the independent and dependent variables? What did the experimenter attempt to control in this study? How was this control achieved?

Do you agree with the conclusions drawn by this researcher? If you had to design a study to test the hypothesis under consideration, how would you design your study? Is your design better than that described above?

MULTIPLE CHOICE

When psychologists use the word behavior they mean
    a.   act right, as in "Behave yourself!"
    b.   observable overt activities of people and animals.
    c.   covert psychological processes.
    d.   both b and c

1.   Covert psychological processes
    a.   can never be studied by psychologists.
    b.   can be observed and measured directly.
    c.   can be studied indirectly by measuring overt behavior.
    d.   are imaginary.

2.   In the demonstration experiment on reading and counting, the fastest condition was
    a.   reading digits
    b.   counting +'s
    c.   counting digits
    d.   there were no differences among these conditions

3. In the demonstration experiment on reading and counting, the slowest condition was
    a. reading digits.
    b. counting +'s.
    c. counting digits.
    d. there were no differences among these conditions

4. Experimental psychologists engage in research
    a. to help develop theoretical understanding of the phenomenon of interest.
    b. to solve practical problems.
    c. because their professor requires it.
    d. two of the above.

5. A critic
    a. makes informed or reasoned judgments.
    b. finds fault with the work of others.
    c. is less objective than an evaluator.
    d. is one who is unable to engage in research directly.

6. In an experiment, the independent variable is
    a. manipulated by the experimenter.
    b. measured by the experimenter.
    c. held constant.
    d. two of the above

7. In an experiment, the dependent variable is
    a. measured by the experimenter.
    b. manipulated by the experimenter.
    c. held constant.
    d. two of the above

8. In an experiment, a control variable is
    a. manipulated by the experimenter.
    b. measured by the experimenter.
    c. held constant.
    d. two of the above

9. When some aspect of an experiment changes along with changes in the independent variable,
    a. you are more likely to get interpretable results.
    b. you are more likely to get large behavioral effects.
    c. confederation has occurred.
    d. confounding has occurred.

10. In the demonstration experiment of the Stroop effect, what was confounded with the levels of the independent variable?
    a.   response time
    b.   task differences
    c.   task ordering
    d.   response ordering

11. Research ideas can come from
    a.   consulting with an expert.
    b.   reading journal articles.
    c.   identifying practical problems.
    d.   all of the above

12. A statement about a presumed or theoretical relationship between two or more variables that includes a description of how these variables are to be measured is called a
    a.   psychological theory.
    b.   research design.
    c.   citation abstract.
    d.   testable hypothesis.

13. In addition to providing research ideas, a literature search is useful in finding out
    a.   if your research hypothesis has already been studied.
    b.   useful "tricks of the trade" in designing your experiment.
    c.   both a and b
    d.   none of the above

14. Preliminary research performed beginning a full-scale experiment
    a.   is called pilot research.
    b.   allows you to get the bugs out of your experimental procedure.
    c.   allows you to identify useful levels of your independent variable.
    d.   all of the above

TRUE-FALSE

_____1. There is no reason to learn about research, unless you personally plan to conduct research.

_____2. It is possible for research findings to be useful, even if they don't increase our theoretical understanding.

_____3. If confounding has occurred, the effect of the independent variable is always overestimated.

_____4. If the same people are all tested under several experimental conditions, testing different people with different orders of these conditions will reduce the condition-order confounding.

_____5. Psychological Abstracts lists the titles of articles from almost all journals that publish psychological research.

_____6. If the variables mentioned in an hypothesis are not measurable, the hypothesis is not testable.

ESSAY QUESTIONS

1. Ask at least three questions based on the Stroop phenomenon. Select one of these questions and discuss each of the steps you might go through in developing a research project to answer this question.

2. Are the same steps involved in developing research to increase theoretical understanding as in developing research to answer a practical question? Explain.

ANSWERS

KEY TERM MATCHING

1. b, a, c   2. a, c, b   3. a, b, d, c   4. a, c, b, f, d, e

PROGRAMMED REVIEW

1. behavior; (p. 4)
2. understanding, practical problems; (p. 7)
3. critic; (p. 9)
4. independent variable; (p. 9)
5. dependent variable; (p. 9)
6. control variables; (p. 9)
7. confounding; (p. 10)
8. observation; (p. 11)

9. experts; (p. 11)
10. *Psychological Abstracts*; (p. 13)
11. testable hypothesis; (p. 13)
12. measurable, related; (p. 13)
13. literature search; (p. 14)
14. pilot; (p.15)

.MULTIPLE CHOICE

1. a; (p. 4)	2. b; (p. 5)	3. a; (p. 5)
4. c; (p. 7)	5. d; (p. 9)	6. a; (p. 9)
7. a; (p. 9)	8. b; (p. 9)	9. c; (p. 10)
10. d; (p. 10)	11. c; (p. 11)	12. d; (p. 13)
13. d; (p. 14)	14. c; (p. 15)	

TRUE-FALSE

1. F; (p. 9)	2. T; (p. 7)	3. F; (p. 10)
4. T; (p. 10)	5. F; (p. 13)	6. T; (p. 13)

CHAPTER 2
Explanation in Scientific Psychology

SUMMARY

I. Methods of fixing belief
    A. Pierce's Nonscientific Methods
        1. **Method of authority**
            a. believing what a trusted source says
            b. simplest method of fixing belief
        2. **Method of tenacity**
            a. maintaining a belief despite evidence to the contrary
        3. **a priori method**
            a. believing something reasonable without prior study
            b. that which is believed is determined by the general cultural outlook
    B. **Scientific Method**
        1. belief is fixed on the basis of experience; it is **empirical**
        2. is **self-correcting**; new empirical evidence can cause old beliefs to be discarded

II. The nature of scientific explanation
    A. Two important elements of science are
        1. **data** - the empirical observations
        2. **theory**
            a. organizes concepts
            b. permits prediction of data
    B. **Induction** and **Deduction**
        1. The inductive approach emphasizes data
            a. science is viewed as working from data to theory
            b. but new techniques and circumstances of observation force these theories to change
        2. The deductive approach emphasizes theory
            a. science is viewed as predicting data from theory

      b.   but
           (1)   correct predictions cannot prove a theory
           (2)   according to Popper's **falsifiability view**, scientifically useful theories are testable and capable of being disproved
           (3)   theories are often limited by including assumptions about the world that are difficult to test and may be wrong
   3.   Induction and deduction are best viewed as complementary rather than in competition

C.   What is a theory?
   1.   A set of related statements that explains a variety of occurrences
      a.   The fewer the statements and the more the occurrences, the better the theory
   2.   The two major functions of a theory are
      a.   to **organize** existing data, and
      b.   to **predict** outcomes of research not yet performed

D.   **Intervening Variables**
   1.   What are they?
      a.   They are abstract concepts; i.e. not directly observable
      b.   They link independent and dependent variables
   2.   When intervening variables are used, theories are simplified in that fewer links are needed to relate independent and dependent variables

E.   Criteria for Evaluating Theories
   1.   **Parsimony**: The fewer the number of statements, the better the theory
   2.   **Precision**: The more exact the predictions, the better the theory
   3.   **Testability**: A good theory can be disproved

III. The Science of Psychology
   A.   Applied research aims at solving specific real-world problems
   B.   Basic research establishes a reservoir of data, theories and concepts
   C.   The results of basic research may find practical application in the future, but it may require a long time, and it is not obvious which basic research will have a future impact

KEY TERM MATCHING

1.

____ a priori method

____ method of authority

____ method of tenacity

____ scientific method

____ what each of the above is

a. a way to fix belief
b. characteristic of bigots
c. empirical and self-correcting
d. the Bible told me so
e. the sun will rise in the east tomorrow

2.

____ applied research

____ basic research

____ data

____ deduction

____ falsifiability view

____ induction

____ strong inference

____ theory

a. aimed at solving a real-world problem
b. aimed at understanding the processes underlying behavior
c. derivation of theory from data
d. empirical observations
e. organizes existing data and predicts new data
f. pitting possible outcomes against each other to decide between competing theories
g. prediction of data from theory
h. useful theories must be capable of being disproved

3.

____ parsimony

____ precision

____ testability

____ what each of the above is

a. can be shown to be false
b. criterion for evaluating a theory
c. the fewer the statements, the better
d. the more exact the prediction, the better

4.

_____ diffusion of responsibility

_____ social loafing

_____ workload

a. an intervening variable
b. people work less hard in a group than when alone
c. a possible reason for b.

PROGRAMMED REVIEW

1. The phenomenon of people working less hard in groups than alone is called
   _____ _____

2. Social loafing may be a special case of a more general social phenomenon called
   _____ of _____ .

3. According to the American philosopher Charles Sanders Pierce, the simplest way of fixing belief is the method of _____ .

4. The method of fixing beliefs in which one refuses to alter their acquired knowledge regardless of evidence to the contrary is known as the method of
   _____ .

5. In the scientific method of fixing beliefs, beliefs are fixed on the basis of
   _____ .

6. Scientific psychology is characterized as being _____ and _____ -correcting.

7. The two most important elements shared by all approaches to science are
   _____ and _____ .

8. In the inductive approach to science, reasoning proceeds from particular _____ to a general _____ . The opposite occurs in the _____ approach to science.

9. The _____ scientist believes that general explanatory principles will emerge once enough data have been collected.

10. According to the _____ approach to theories, data are useful only in the evaluation of a theoretical explanation.

11. According to Popper, the philosopher of science, good theories must be
    _____ .

12. Experiments designed to pit two hypotheses against each other in the hope of eliminating one of them involve the process of _____ _____.

13. One function of a theory is to provide a framework for _____ existing data.

14. Theories may be used to generate _____ for situations where no data have yet been obtained.

15. The two functions of a theory known as organization and prediction are sometimes called _____ and _____, respectively.

16. An abstract concept that relates independent and dependent variables is called an _____ _____.

17. Intervening variables, by reducing the number of links necessary to relate independent and dependent variables, provide _____ in explanation.

18. A good theory will make very _____ predictions.

19. In evaluating theories, the criterion of _____ holds that the fewer the concepts a theory needs to explain various phenomena, the better the theory.

20. Theories having mathematical formulations are said to have greater _____ than those using only verbal statements.

21. A theory that cannot be _____ can never be disproved.

22. What distinguishes one science from another is the different _____ that are used.

23. Psychologists try to understand the underlying _____ that lead to behavior rather than the physical situations that produce behaviors.

EXPERIMENTAL PROJECT

Suppose that someone comes to you with an infinitely large deck of cards. Each card contains a geometric shape (circle, square, or triangle) on one side and a color patch (red, green, or yellow) on the other. The person with the cards tells you that each card with a circle on one side has either a green or a blue patch on the other side. Your task is to test this "theory" in any way you wish, with the restriction that you may only turn over one card at a time. What sort of "evidence" would you consider critical in testing this theory? How many cards would you need to see before you believed the theory? Would your answer to these questions change if the person stated that 9 out of 10 cards with a circle on one side have a green or blue patch on the other side?

EXPERIMENTAL DILLEMA

Two researchers are studying the effects of marijuana on personal motivation. Both experimenters believe that chronic marijuana use is associated with a decline in motivation level, but they have different ways of studying the problem. Research A hypothesizes that "Grade point average decreases logarithmically with the number of marijuana cigarettes smoked per week." Researcher B's hypothesis states that "People who smoke marijuana have less drive to succeed than people who do not smoke marijuana." Which experimenter has a better research hypothesis? Why?

MULTIPLE CHOICE

1. The tendency of people to work less hard in groups is known as
   a. diffusion of effort.
   b. social irresponsibility.
   c. social loafing.
   d. good sense.

2. Experiments have shown that people work just as hard in a group as when they work alone if
   a. good performance is rewarded.
   b. team spirit" is high.
   c. the group leader is autocratic.
   d. each individual's performance is monitored.

3. The simplest way of fixing beliefs is
   a. the a priori method.
   b. the method of authority.
   c. the method of tenacity.
   d. the scientific method.

4. After listening to a lecture by an astronaut who conducted experiments aboard the space shuttle, you now believe that plants can germinate in space. This belief was fixed by
   a. the method of authority.
   b. the method of tenacity.
   c. the scientific method.
   d. the empirical method.

5. Your roommate asks whether you believe that sunbathing can increase one's chances of getting skin cancer. You reply that of course it can because "baking in the sun is bound to be harmful to skin tissue." This belief was probably fixed by
   a. the a priori method.
   b. he method of authority.
   c. the scientific method.
   d. the method of tenacity.

6. Fixing belief a priori refers to
   a. appealing to higher authorities.
   b. believing views that seem reasonable.
   c. believing opinions based on systematic observation.
   d. believing only facts and not unsupported opinions.

7. A disadvantage of fixing beliefs by the method of authority or a priori is that
   a. neither method involves systematic observation.
   b. neither method offers a way of deciding which of two beliefs is superior to the other.
   c. neither method results in beliefs that are precise or testable.
   d. both a and b

8. The scientific method is the preferred technique for satisfying curiosity because it
   a. relies on systematic observation.
   b. is self-correcting.
   c. provides an empirical basis for fixing belief.
   d. all of the above

9. The _____ scientist emphasizes data and the _____ scientist emphasizes theory.
   a. inductive; deductive
   b. empirical; inductive
   c. deductive; inductive
   d. deductive; empirical

10. The inductive scientist
   a. conducts research in order to gain support for a particular theoretical view.
   b. believes that organized patterns of important empirical relations will emerge once enough data are collected.
   c. is not concerned with empirical observation.
   d. none of the above

11. The deductive scientist
    a.   conducts research in order to gain support for a particular theoretical view.
    b.   believes that organizational patterns will emerge once enough data are collected.
    c.   is concerned primarily with empirical observation.
    d.   none of the above

12. Which of the following is true concerning inductive and deductive scientists?
    a.   Inductive scientists are more important because they provide basic data upon which to build theories.
    b.   Deductive scientists are more important because they try to bring order out of the mass of data collected by empiricists.
    c.   Most psychologists take either a purely inductive or purely deductive approach.
    d.   none of the above

13. According to the falsifiability view of theories proposed by Popper, _____ in evaluating a theory.
    a.   negative evidence is more important than positive evidence
    b.   positive evidence is more important than negative evidence
    c.   replications of theories is most important
    d.   proving the unreliability of a theory is most important

14. One key aspect of the falsifiability view of theories is that falsifiability depends upon _____.
    a.   fabricating data
    b.   unreliable data
    c.   empirical observations
    d.   theoretical deductions

15. Which of the following procedures should, in the ideal case, yield one theory if the process is used repeatedly?
    a.   deductive reasoning
    b.   inductive reasoning
    c.   hypothesis testing
    d.   strong inference

16. Theories
    a.   serve to organize existing data.
    b.   generate predictions for situations where no data have yet been collected.
    c.   can never be proven to be true.
    d.   all of the above

17. Intervening variables serve to connect
    a. data and theory.
    b. hypothesis and experiment.
    c. independent and dependent variables.
    d. deduction and induction.

18. Inclusion of intervening variables may make a theory more
    a. precise.
    b. testable.
    c. parsimonious.
    d. valid.

19. Theories with mathematical formulations are said to be more _____ than verbal theories.
    a. parsimonious
    b. correct
    c. precise
    d. provable

20. If a theory is not _____ if it can never be disproved.
    a. parsimonious
    b. precise
    c. testable
    d. mathematical

21. Which of the following is true?
    a. Data that are partially consistent with a theory can cause the theory to be modified.
    b. Data that are inconsistent with a theory can lead to the rejection of that theory.
    c. Data that are consistent with a theory can never prove the theory.
    d. All of the above.

22. A scientist theorizes that if all males were removed from society the incidence of violent crime would decrease by at least 80%. The major problem with this hypotheses is that it is not _____.
    a. precise
    b. testable
    c. parsimonious
    d. reliable

23. If a theory cannot be potentially disproved
    a. it is said to be unparsimonious.
    b. it is said to be testable.
    c. it is useless to scientists.
    d. none of the above

24. The fact that the relationship between basic psychological research and pressing social issues is not immediately obvious
    a. suggests that psychology has little to offer in the way of improving society.
    b. does not mean that no such relationship actually exists.
    c. means that federal funding should be withheld from psychological research.
    d. suggests that psychologists are studying the wrong problems.

25. Psychologists
    a. are more interested in physical situations that produce behavior rather than in the underlying process.
    b. are interested in neither physical situations nor underlying processes that produce behavior.
    c. are more interested in underlying processes that produce behavior than in physical situations.
    d. none of the above

TRUE-FALSE

____ 1. The method of authority involves taking someone else's word on faith.

____ 2. Religious beliefs are generally formed by the method of tenacity.

____ 3. An advantage of the scientific method over other methods of fixing beliefs is that it offers a means of determining the "superiority" of one belief over another.

____ 4. Scientific data are necessarily empirical observations.

____ 5. All approaches to science involve data and theory.

____ 6. According to the inductive approach to science, general explanations are arrived at from a set of theoretical statements that can then be tested against data.

____ 7. Theories induced from empirical observations are tentative due to the limited scope of the available data.

____ 8. Deductive approaches to science emphasize the primacy, or primary role, of theory.

____ 9. Many correct predictions made by a theory can help to prove the theory to be correct.

____ 10. A theory may never be proved.

____ 11. The purposes of a psychological theory are to describe and explain behavior.

____ 12. Intervening variables serve to link observables to non-observables.

____ 13. Inclusion of intervening variables makes theories less parsimonious than they would otherwise be.

____ 14. If two theories can account for the same data, but Theory A uses 10 statements and Theory B uses 15, then Theory B is the better theory.

____ 15. One function of a scientific theory is to allow scientists to generate predictions for situations where no data have yet been obtained.

____ 16. Verbal theories are generally considered useless in psychology.

____ 17. The criterion of parsimony is most concerned with the number of findings a theory can account for.

____ 18. A theory may be precise without being testable.

____ 19. Applied research inevitably precedes basic research.

____ 20. According to the text, the inability to predict which basic research being done today will have an impact on society years from now means that we should stop doing basic research.

____ 21. Basic researchers generally assume that different mental processes occurs across different physical situations.

____ 22. Establishing similar physical situations in which to observe behavior guarantees similarity in the mental processes underlying the behaviors.

ESSAY QUESTIONS

____ 1. What are three methods for fixing belief? Which of these methods is superior to the others and why?

____ 2. What are the advantages and disadvantages of the inductive and deductive approaches to science? Can either of these approaches be said to be the better of the two? Why or why not?

____ 3. What is meant by basic research and applied research? Are the two endeavors related or separate enterprises?

___ 4. What criteria may be used to evaluate theories? Which of these is the most crucial and why?

ANSWERS

KEY TERM MATCHING

1. e, d, c, b, a   2. a, b, d, g, h, c, f, e   3. c, d, a, b   4. c, b, a

PROGRAMMED REVIEW

1. social loafing; (p. 30)
2. diffusion of responsibility; (p. 31)
3. authority; (p. 32)
4. tenacity; (p. 32)
5. observation; (p. 33)
6. empirical, self; (p. 33)
7. empirical, self-correcting; (p. 33)
8. observation, theory, deductive; (p. 34)
9. inductive; (p. 34)
10. deductive; (p. 35)
11. falsifiable; (p.35)
12. strong inference; (p. 37)
13. organizing; (p. 37)
14. predictions; (p. 37)
15. description, explanation; (p. 38)
16. intervening variable; (p. 39)
17. economy; (p. 42)
18. precise; (p. 43)
19. parsimony; (p. 42)
20. precision; (p. 43)
21. tested; (p. 43)
22. techniques; (p. 44)
23. processes; (p. 46)

MULTIPLE CHOICE

1. c; (p. 30)	2. d; (p. 31)	3. b; (p. 32)
4. a; (p. 32)	5. a; (p. 32)	6. b; (p. 32)
7. d; (p. 33)	8. d; (p. 33)	9. a; (p. 34)
10. b; (p. 34)	11. a; (p. 34)	12. d; (p. 35)
13. a; (p. 35)	14. c; (p. 35)	15. d; (p. 37)
16. d; (p. 37)	17. c; (p. 39)	18. c; (p. 43)
19. c; (p. 43)	20. c; (p. 43)	21. d; (p. 43)
22. b; (p. 43)	23. c; (p. 43)	24. b; (p. 45)
25. c; (p. 46)		

TRUE-FALSE

1. T; (p. 32)	2. F; (p. 32)	3. T; (p. 33)
4. T; (p. 33)	5. T; (p. 34)	6. F; (p. 34)
7. T; (p. 35)	8. T; (p. 34)	9. F; (p. 35)
10. T; (p. 35)	11. T; (p. 37)	12. F; (p. 39)
13. F; (p. 42)	14. F; (p. 42)	15. T; (p. 37)
16. T; (p. 43)	17. F; (p. 42)	18. F; (p. 43)
19. F; (p. 45)	20. F; (p. 46)	21. F; (p. 46)
22. F; (p. 46)		

CHAPTER 3.

Observation in Psychological Research

Summary

I.   Valid Observations
      A.   The **validity** of observations is essential for the ways that observations provide scientific understanding:
            1.   **Descriptive observations** describe behavior
            2.   **Relational observations** relate two or more behaviors
            3.   **Explanation** indentifies the causes of behavior
      B.   **Construct Validity**
            1.   refers to the degree to which the independent and dependent variables accurately reflect what is intended.
            2.   Two threats to construct validity are
                  a.   confounding
                  b.   random error
            3.   Construct invalidity may be minimized by using
                  a.   **operational definitions** - recipes for producing and measuring constructs
                  b.   **protocols** - plans for the treatment of subjects that specify for how measurements are to be undertaken
      C.   **External Validity**
            1.   refers to the extent that one can generalize from the research setting and samples to other settings and populations.
            2.   External validity is established through replication of research under different circumstances.

D. **Internal Validity**
   1. refers to whether one can decide that changes in dependent variables were caused by changes in independent variables.
   2. In principle, experimental observations permit causal statements; experiments provide greater internal validity than other observational techniques.
   3. Confounding is a major threat to interval validity.

II. Descriptive Observation Methods
   A. The Methods
      1. **Naturalistic Observations**
         a. refers to direct observations of behavior, usually in the natural enviroment.
         b. An important initial problem to be solved is limiting and specifying the range of behaviors to be recorded
         c. **Ethology** is the study of naturally occurring behavior, often in the wild.
            (1) Ethologists make use of ethograms to make more systematic observations
            (2) **Ethograms** are inventories of various actions that are produced by a particular species when engaged in a particular (broad) category of behavior.
            (3) **Interobserver reliability** indicates the degree of agreement between two or more observers, and is usually measured by a correlation coefficient.
      2. The **Case Study**
         a. refers to an intensive investigation of a single case of some sort.
         b. Case studies usually do not allow firm inferences about what causes what.
         c. A **deviant-case analysis** is a type of case study that compares two cases with many similarities but with different outcomes, thereby strengthening causal inferences.
      3. **Survey Research**
         a. refers to research in which a small amount of data is collected (often from questionnaires) from many subjects that are (usually) respresentative of the larger population.
         b. Stratfied samples are often used in survey research, in which the proportions of sample mirror the proportions of the population for characteristics believed to be important.

4. **Meta-Analysis**
    a.   refers to a relatively objective technique for summarizing across many studies that investigate a single topic.
    b.   allows the external validity of an experimental factor to be determined, as well as its relative strength.

B.   Advantages of Descriptive Observation
    1.   They are useful in early stages of research for
        a.   studying the breadth and range of the problem
        b.   raising interesting questions for more controlled research
    2.   They typically study interesting naturally occurring behaviors that may suggest the **ecological function** of various behaviors, i.e. how these behaviors help the organism adapt to the environment.
    3.   They often provide a high **ecological validity**; observations are made in real-world and not artificial settings.

C.   Sources of Error in Descriptive Research
    1.   The primary problem is that descriptive research does not allow the assessment of *relations* among events.
    2.   Decriptive research (especially the case study) is often not readily reproducable by other researchers
    3.   When presenting results, it is difficult to remain at the descriptive, and not the interpretative level. In particular, **anthropomorphizing**, attributing human characteristics to animals, is difficult to avoid in naturalistic observation.

D.   Reactivity in Descriptive Research
    1.   **Reactivity** refers to the influence of the observational procedure on the behavior being observed.
        a.   **Subject roles** is a term that highlights the social and psychological factors present in a research situation that may influence the results.
        b.   Demand Characteristics is an older term that emphasizes the obedience of a subject to the researcher's demands.
    2.   In naturalistic observation, reactivity can be reduced by
        a.   **Unobtrusive observations**, in which subjects are unaware that they are being observed. This can be accomplished by
            (1)   special apparatus (camoflague, sideways camera lenses, etc.)
            (2)   **participant observation** in which the researcher becomes a part of the of subject's natural enviornment

      b.   **Unobtrusive Measures**, in which the behavior is observed indirectly by examining the results of behavior that has already occurred.

   3.   In case studies much of the data is **retrospective** - it comes from looking in the past

      a.   This data may be inaccurate due to ordinary forgetting.

      b.   **Motivated forgetting** occurs when people reconstruct their past experiences to match their current beliefs.

   4.   In Surveys, interviews and tests data may be distorted by

      a.   the **response style** of the subject - an habitual way of answering questions

         (1)   response styles include:

            (a)   **response acquiescence** - a tendency to agree with questions

            (b)   **response deviation** - a tendency to disagree with question

            (c)   **social desirability** - a tendency to give a socially desirable response

         (2)   the problem of response styles and be reduced by using a **forced-choice test** in which the subject must select between two alternatives of equal social desirability

      b.   the **volunteer problem** - people who volunteer to participate in research differ in many ways from people who do not volunteer

KEY TERM MATCHING

1.

____descriptive observation

____meta-analysis

____naturalistic observation

____participant observation

____relational observation

____unobtrusive observation

a. observing how two or more behaviors go together

b. determines the external validity of a treatment by examining many studies

c. includes naturalistic observation, case studies and surveys

d. most apt to be done by an ethologist

e. non-reactive direct observation of behavior

f. one way to study mountain gorillas

2.

___construct validity

___ecological validity

___interobserver reliability

___internal validity

___validity

a. degree to which independent observers agree
b. degree to which the observational environment is true of the real world
c. degree to which variables accurately reflect what they are intended to measure
d. degree to which we can be sure that experimental results are produced by the independent variable
e. soundness or truth of observations

3.

___response acquiescence

___response styles

___response deviation

___social desirability

___subject roles

a. response habits in answering questions
b. social and psychological factors that might influence research results
c. tendency to give a "no" answer
d. tendency to give a "yes" answer
e. tendency to give a socially acceptable answer

4.

___anthropomorphizing

___case study

___demand characteristics

___ethology

___reactivity

___retrospective

___survey

___volunteer problem

a. a small amount of data is gathered from a large sample
b. attributing human characteristics to animals
c. derived from participant's memory
d. intensive investigation of a single individual case of interest
e. older term for subject reactivity
f. people willing to participate in research are different from those unwilling to participate
g. study of behavior in the natural environment
h. the act of observing behavior affects the behavior

5.

___deviant case analysis

___forced-choice test

___protocol

___replication

___ethogram

a. a varient of the case study method that strengthens causal inference
b. catalogue of actions of a species associated with a particular type of behavior
c. means of establishing external validity
d. means to ensure that all subjects are treated similarly in a study
e. means to reduce the response-style problem

Programmed Review

1. The _____ of an observation refers to its truth.

2. _____ validity refers to the extent that a variable is an appropriate and accurate measure of whatever the variable represents.

3. _____ and _____ _____ are possible threats to construct validity.

4. An _____ _____ is a recipe that specifies how a construct is produced and measured in an experiment. Use of these helps to minimize _____ invalidity.

5. A _____ is a precise specification of how the measurement of behavior is to be undertaken.

6. _____ validity refers to the extent that research can be generalized to other settings and subject populations.

7. If we wanted to demonstrate that findings of a particular experiment had external validity, we should _____ the study under altered conditions.

8. The ability to claim that changes in behavior are caused by manipulation of the independent variable refers to _____ _____.

9. The major threat to internal validity is _____.

10. _____ observations enumerate what behaviors occur and in what quantity and frequency.

11. Examples of descriptive observations include _____ _____, the _____ _____ and _____.

12. Descriptive observations are a useful first step in research since they provide and extend the _____ that can lead to more controlled experimentation.

13. Descriptive observations alone can not tell us how events are _____ to each other.

14. Descriptive observation, in particular the case study, is limited because the observations often cannot be _____.

15. _____ is the study of naturally occurring behavior (often in the wild).

16. A(n) _____ is a inventory of specific actions that a particular species might produce in one behavioral category.

17. _____ _____ refers to the agreement between two independent observers of the same behavior.

18. A(n)_____ _____ is an intensive investigation of a single case or some sort.

19. The _____-_____ _____ compares two individuals who are similar in many characteristics, but have different outcomes.

20. In _____ research, a small amount of data is collected from a large sample of people.

21. A(n) _____ _____ is a group of subjects that is constructed to mirror the proportional membership in various categories that exists in the population.

22. A _____-_____ seeks to determine the external validity of a treatment by examining many research studies of that treatment.

23. It is difficult to maintain a descriptive rather than interpretative level of observation, for example, avoiding _____, the attribution of human characteristics to animals.

24. In principle, _____ observation allows us to infer causality, because by manipulating the independent variable, and holding other variables constant, we know the direction of the effect.

25. When the process of observing behavior changes that behavior, the process is said to be _____.

26. Two general ways to guard against participant's reactions from ruining our research is to make unobtrusive _____ or make unobtrusive _____.

27. Unobtrusive measures are _____ observations of behavior.

28. _____ _____ is a way of making unobtrusive observations by gaining acceptance of the observed subjects.

29. Much of the evidence in a case study is _____ in nature.

30. A problem inherent in case studies is _____ _____: People often distort unpleasant events.

31. Tests and survey results may be contaminated by response _____ or _____ sets.

32. The forced-choice technique requires subjects to select between two alternative of equal _____ _____.

33. One problem inherent in interpreting data from opinion surveys that rely on volunteer mailings is the _____ _____.

EXPERIMENTAL PROJECT

You have probably noticed that many people who park in spaced reserved for the handicapped do not appear to be handicapped when they leave their cars. Most states provide specially labeled license plates for handicapped drivers. Decide on some characteristics that you think might be related to this kind of behavior. You might, for example, decide that drivers of a particular sex, age group, or those that drive particular kinds of vehicles are more likely to engage in this antisocial behavior. Decide what *you* think might be interesting to investigate, and develop an organized way of recording your observations. Finally, visit a parking lot that services a wide variety of people, and collect your data. Your instructor will assist you in analyzing the data.

EXPERIMENTAL DILEMMA

Several years ago, television ratings were determined quite differently than they are today. A carefully constructed stratified sample of households with television sets were provided with meters that were attached to the TV sets and recorded when the sets were on, and which station to sets were tuned to. Why was this practice abandoned?

MULTIPLE CHOICE

1. We have confidence that our psychological descriptions, relationships, and explanations are good when they are based on
    a. testable hypotheses.
    b. valid observations.
    c. useful research.
    d. all of the above

2. The degree to which independent and dependent variables accurately reflect or measure what they are intended to measure is
    a. construct validity.
    b. external validity.
    c. internal validity.
    d. predictive validity.

3. If a subject were apprehensive about being in an experiment, it is likely that time to read a passage would lack _____ _____ as a measure of reading skill.
    a. construct validity
    b. external validity
    c. internal validity
    d. predictive validity

4. A specification of the conditions that would be used to produce anxiety in experimental subjects, and of the way that this anxiety would be measured, constitute a _____ of anxiety.
    a. external validation procedure
    b. internal validation procedure
    c. operational definition
    d. protocol

5. The use of protocols and operational definitions is useful in reducing _____ invalidity.
    a. construct
    b. external
    c. internal
    d. predictive

6. The extent to which research findings can be generalized to other populations and settings refers to
   a. construct validity.
   b. external validity.
   c. internal validity.
   d. predictive validity.

7. Replicating experiments using different tasks, different experimental settings, or with different subject populations helps to establish
   a. construct validity.
   b. external validity.
   c. internal validity.
   d. predictive validity.

8. Whether or not we can claim that changes in the independent variable caused changes to occur in the dependent variable refers to
   a. construct validity.
   b. external validity.
   c. internal validity.
   d. predictive validity.

9. Confounding in an experiment threatens
   a. construct validity.
   b. external validity.
   c. internal validity.
   d. predictive validity.

10. The advantage of descriptive observation is that
    a. it allows for a good deal of experimental control.
    b. it allows for easy replication.
    c. it helps to define a problem area and raise interesting questions.
    d. it is primarily concerned with relationships.

11. A relatively complete inventory of specific behaviors performed by one species of animal, and that is useful in naturalistic observation is a
    a. ethogram.
    b. response catalog.
    c. survey.
    d. protocol.

12. An intensive investigation of a particular person, or a particular group of people is called
    a. a case study.
    b. an ethogram.
    c. relational research.
    d. a survey.

13. In a deviant-case analysis, the researcher
    a. conducts an intensive investigation of an unusual individual.
    b. conducts naturalistic observations in an environment populated by deviants.
    c. investigates the relationships of an unusual person.
    d. considers two cases with many similarities but that differ in the outcome.

14. When you brought a new puppy home, your old dog Spot bit you on the ankle. Calling Spot 'jealous' is an example of
    a. anthropomorphism.
    b. a deviant-case study.
    c. naturalistic observation.
    d. concept validity.

15. The primary problem unique to descriptive observation is that it
    a. does not allow us to assess the relations among events.
    b. suffers from external invalidity.
    c. is only concerned with deviant cases.
    d. can not be quantified.

16. Unobtrusive measures are
    a. direct observations taken without the awareness of the individual(s) being observed.
    b. indirect observations of behavior.
    c. obtained through participant observation.
    d. best avoided in naturalistic observations.

17. Which of the following does not pose a problem when attempting to interpret the results of a case study?
    a. the evidence is retrospective
    b. memory is fallible
    c. incomplete records
    d. none of the above

18. In meta-analysis, many studies of the same treatment are examined in order to determine the
    a. relative effectiveness of the treatment
    b. internal validity of the treatment effects
    c. external validity of the treatment effects
    d. both a and b
    e. both a and c
    f. both b and c

19. Which of the following is not a type of response style?
    a. response acquiescence
    b. response deviation
    c. social adaptability
    d. social desirability

20. A forced choice test procedure is an effort to
    a. avoid response-style problems.
    b. avoid motivated forgetting.
    c. solve the volunteer problem.
    d. remove demand characteristics.

21. Subject reactivity refers to the problem of
    a. subjects misinterpreting the experimenter's instructions.
    b. the influence of the expectations of the experimenter on the experimental results.
    c. the subjects' behavior being influenced by being in an experiment.
    d. treatment carryover effects.

22. Reactivity can be minimized in observational research by
    a. using a double-blind procedure.
    b. using obtrusive measures.
    c. employing a placebo.
    d. participant observation.

23. Response style refers to
    a. demand characteristics in field research.
    b. reconstructive processes in retrospective memory.
    c. a habitual way of answering a question.
    d. a source of reactivity in interviewing and surveys.
    e. both c and d

24. The "volunteer problem" refers to
    a. the problem associated with getting people to participate in psychological experiments.
    b. people who volunteer differ in many ways from people who do not volunteer.
    c. the ethics of using volunteers in experimentation.
    d. identifying a sample of people who are likely to volunteer for an experiment.

TRUE FALSE

____1. Validity and invalidity refer to the best approximation to the truth or falsity of propositions.

____2. Amount of hair, as a measure of intelligence, would seem to lack external validity.

____3. Random error is a major threat to the internal validity of an observation.

____4. Protocols are more precise than operational definitions.

____5. Research findings that are only true of a particular strain of white rats would seem to lack predictive validity.

____6. Construct validity can be demonstrated by replicating an experiment with different tasks.

____7. In principle, experimental observations permit causal statements.

____8. Imprecise protocols are the major threat to internal validity.

____9. Naturalistic observation is inherently unsystematic in the way that data is collected.

____10. The text suggests than descriptive observation is not inferior to, but simply prior to experimentation.

____11. Ethology refers to the study of naturally occurring behavior (often in the wild).

____12. Eibl-Eibesfeldt's research on the eyebrow flash is a good use of the survey technique.

___13. Lovelace and Twohig used a survey to demonstrate that younger and older people used different strategies to remember things.

___14. While external validity may be questionable, descriptive observation guarantees internal and construct validity.

ESSAY QUESTIONS

1. Discuss how confounding can reduce both construct and internal validity.

2. Discuss the advantages and disadvantages of naturalistic observation.

3. What additional power is provided by a deviant-case study over an ordinary case study?

ANSWERS

KEY TERM MATCHING

1. c, b, d, f, a, e
2   c, b, a, d, e
3. d, a, c, e, b
4. b, d, e, g, h, c, a, f

PROGRAMMED REVIEW

1. validity; (p. 53)
2. construct; (p. 55)
3. confounding, random error; (p. 56)
4. operational definition; (p. 56)
5. protocol; (p. 57)
6. external ; (p. 57)
7. replicate; (p. 57)
8. internal validity; (p. 58)
9. confounding; (p. 58)
10. descriptive; (p. 59)
11. naturalistic observations, case study, survey; (p. 59)
12. database; (p. 61)
13. related; (p. 71)
14. reproduced; (p. 73)
15. ethology; (p. 62)
16. ethogram; (p. 63)
17. interobserver reliability; (p. 64)
18. case study; (p. 65)
19. deviant-case analysis; (p. 66)

20. survey; (p. 67)
21. stratified sample; (p. 68)
22. meta-analysis; (p. 68)
23. anthropomorphism; (p. 73)
24. experimental; (p. 72)
25. reactive; (p. 73)
26. observations, measurements; (p. 74)
27. indirect; (p. 75)
28. participant observation; (p. 74)
29. retrospective; (p. 75)
30. motivated forgetting; (p. 75)
31. style, response; (p. 76)
32. social desirability; (p. 76)
33. volunteer problem; (p. 76)

MULTIPLE CHOICE

1. b; (p. 53)	2. a; (p. 55)	3. a; (p. 55)
4. c; (p. 56)	5. a; (p. 57)	6. b; (p. 57)
7. b; (p. 57)	8. b; (p. 58)	9. c; (p. 59)
10. c; (p. 59)	11. a; (p. 63)	12. a; (p. 65)
13. d; (p. 66)	14. a; (p. 73)	15. a; (p. 72)
16. b; (p. 75)	17. d; (p. 75)	18. e; (p. 68)
19. c; (p. 76)	20. a; (p. 76)	21. c; (p. 73)
22. d; (p.74)	23. e; (p. 76)	24. b; (p. 76)

TRUE FALSE

1. T ; (p. 53)	2. F; (p. 55)	3. F; (p. 57)
4. T; (p. 57)	5. F; (p. 58)	6. F; (p. 56)
7. T; (p. 58)	8. F; (p. 57)	9. F; (p. 62)
10. T; (p. 62)	11. T; (p. 62)	12. F; (p. 64)
13. T; (p. 67)	14. F; (p. 71)	

CHAPTER 4.

Relational Research

SUMMARY

I. **Relational Research**
   A. seeks to determine whether and how two or more variables are related
   B. usually does not involve manipulation of variables, so data are **ex post facto**, i.e. measured after the fact of whatever produced them.

II. Contingency Table Research
   A. Contingency tables
      1. A **contingency table** consists of two or more rows and two or more columns, where each row represents a category of one variable, and each column is a category of another variable.
      2. A **cell** is a combination of a row category and a column category.
      3. A contingency table shows how many observations fall into each cell.
   B. Contingency tables are usually analyzed with the X^2 **test for independence**. If the value of X^2 is statistically significant, we can be reasonable sure that the two variables are related.
   C. Contingency table research is most often used with nominal level measurements.
   D. Subject reactivity can be a problem with contingency table research. Since the data are ex post facto, subject reactivity is likely to be from an unknown source, and be of an unknown magnitude.

III. Correlational Research
   A. **The Correlation Coefficient**
      1. usually ranges from -1.0 through 0.0 to +1.00

2. The *magnitude* of the coefficient indicates the strength of the relationship.
3. The *sign* of the of the coefficient indicates the direction of the relationship
   a. positive values indicate positive relationships; as scores on one variable increase, so do scores on the other variable.
   b. negative values indicate negative relationships; high scores on one variable tend to be associated with low scores on the other.
4. The most commonly used correlation coefficient is **Pearson's product-moment correlation coefficient**, or **Pearson's *r***
5. Scatter diagrams are graphs that plot one variable on the abscissa, the other on the ordinate. An individual is represented by a point that shows his scores on both variables
6. Interpreting Correlation Coefficients
   a. correlations do *not* imply a causative relationship between the two variables. If A and B are correlated, we cannot tell whether
      (1) A caused B
      (2) B caused A
      (3) both A and B were caused by a third variable.
7. Low correlations can arise from
   a. a **truncated range** of values on one or both of the variables
   b. using *r* to measure a relationship that is not linear.

B. Complex Correlational Procedures
1. The internal validity of correlational research can be enhanced by examining *patterns* of correlations.
2. The **cross-lagged-panel correlation procedure**
   a. obtains several correlations over time
   b. considers the size and direction of the in order to determine likely causal relationships.

IV. Experimentation and Internal Validity
A. Experimentation involves the manipulation of an independent variable
B. The manipulation allows us to know the direction of the relationship between dependent and independent variables.
C. If we know the direction of the relationship, we can identify the **proximal causes**, or the immediate causes of a behavioral event.

KEY TERM MATCHING

1.

___contingency table

___correlational research

___ex post facto

___proximal causes

___relational research

a. allows researcher to determined both the magnitude and direction of a relationship
b. data are collected after the fact of whatever produced them
c. immediate causes of a behavioral effect
d. includes both contingency table and correlational research
e. shows how often observations fall in each category combination

2.

___X^2 text for independence

___cell

___correlation coefficient

___cross-lagged panel

___Pearson r

___scatter diagram

___truncated rang

a. a graphical means of portraying correlational data
b. combination of categories from each of two variables
c. measures the strength and direction of a relationship
d. one reason why r might be artificially low
e. patterns of correlations are examined over time
f. the most common correlation coefficient
g. used to analyze contingency tables

PROGRAMMED REVIEW

1. _____ _____ attempts to determine how two variables are related.

2. _____ _____ are often used to determine whether two nominal variables are related.

3. In a contingency table, a _____ refers to a combination of a row variable category and a column variable category

4. Contingency tables show the _____ with which observations fall into each cell.

5. The _____ test for _____ is often used to analyze contingency table data.

6. In correlational research, both the _____ and the _____ of a relationship can be determined.

7. Relational research uses a _____ _____ to indicate the degree of relationship between two variables.

8. If two variables are related, we can use knowledge of one variable to _____ the other.

9. Most measures of correlation range in value from _____ to _____.

10. The larger the absolute value of the correlation coefficient, the _____ the relationship.

11. The sign of the correlation coefficient tells us the _____ of the relationship between two variables.

12. A _____ _____ is a kind of graph commonly used to present correlational data.

13. We are not entitled to infer a _____ relationship between two variables, solely on the basis of correlational evidence.

14. The reason that variable A is correlated with variable B might be that A is the cause of B, B is the cause of A, or that both A and B are caused by an unknown _____ _____.

15. Correlation coefficients may be artificially _____ if the range of either variable is restricted.

16. The use of the _____-_____-_____ correlational procedure provides greater internal validity than is provided by the traditional correlational approach.

17. In principle, _____ observation allows us to infer causality, because by manipulating the independent variable, and holding other variables constant, we know the direction of the effect.

EXPERIMENTAL PROJECT

Some psychologists have suggested that there may be a relationship between birth order and intelligence, with first-born children being more intelligent than their younger siblings. In fact, it has been shown that intelligence scores decline steadily with birth order. You can test this hypothesis in the following way. Obtain the number of older siblings that a person has, and let this be the X score. Then let that person's grade point average be his or her Y score. (We are assuming that grade point average is an indicant of intelligence.) Obtain these same measurements from several individuals. You may query as few as 10 people, but it is preferable to have a larger sample size (n) of 25 or so. You might want to pool your data with that collected by other members of the class. Correlate the scores using the Pearson correlation formula found in the text. If the hypothesis is correct, you should obtain a negative correlation with grade point average decreasing as the number of older siblings increases. Do your results support the hypothesis? If not, what reasons can you offer for the discrepancy? What are the implications of your findings? How might you use a contingency table to address the same question?

EXPERIMENTAL DILEMMAS

1.   An industrial psychologist interested in the effects of a work training program on job performance reported the following study. Fifty garment factory workers were given on the job training in a program that lasted either one or two weeks. Afterward their performance in terms of number of work pieces completed in one day was correlated with the number of weeks spent in training. The Pearson coefficient obtained between these two measures was -.02. From this result the researcher concluded that the work training program was ineffective and should be abandoned. If you were a top management executive, would you comply with the researcher's suggestion? If not, why?

2.   A social psychologist interested in the effects of unemployment on alcohol abuse conducted the following study. She mailed questionnaires to the homes of workers who had been laid off from a local automobile plant. The questionnaires were mailed at various time intervals and the workers were asked to fill them out anonymously and to return them. Fifty percent of the questionnaires were completed and returned. For those individuals who returned the questionnaires, the correlation between alcohol consumption and length of unemployment was found to be +.64. That is, more alcohol was consumed as the period of unemployment progressed. In her report the researcher stated that "the conditions of unemployment produce a tendency for people to increase their alcohol intake." If you were the editor in charge of deciding whether this work would be accepted for publication, what would your judgment be?

MULTIPLE CHOICE

1. Relational research is undertaken to
    a. determine proximal causes.
    b. determine ultimate causes.
    c. identify how variables are related.
    d. explain one variable in terms of another

2. Contingency table research is usually done when the data are
    a. nominal
    b. ordinal
    c. interval
    d. ratio

3. A contingency table must have at least _____ row(s) and _____ columns.
    a. 1, 1
    b. 1, 2
    c. 2, 1
    d. 2, 2

4. The various rows in a contingency table represent
    a. different variables.
    b. different categories of the same variable.
    c. different categories of different variables.
    d. relative frequencies of observations.

5. The rows and columns of a contingency table
    a. are different variables.
    b. are different categories of the same variable.
    c. must be the same in number.
    d. must be different in number.

6. The cells in a contingency table
    a. represent combinations of row and column categories.
    b. contain the frequency with which observations fall into category combinations.
    c. contain the average scores made by people in various category combinations.
    d. both *a* and *b*
    e. both *a* and *c*

7. Data in a contingency table are usually analyzed with a
   a. X^2 for dependence
   b. X^2 for independence
   c. Pearson's r
   d. either a or b but not c

8. The use of correlational techniques permits the researcher to
   a. make predictions on the basis of the obtained results.
   b. understand why two variables are related.
   c. manipulate the effect of one variable on another.
   d. infer a lack of causation.

9. When r is positive
   a. high scores on one variable tend to go with high scores on the other
   b. high scores on one variable tend to go with low scores on the other
   c. low scores on one variable tend to go with low scores on the other
   d. both a and c

10. When r is negative
    a. high scores on one variable tend to go with high scores on the other
    b. high scores on one variable tend to go with low scores on the other
    c. low scores on one variable tend to go with low scores on the other
    d. both a and c

11. When there is a strong positive relationship
    a. r is just less than 0.0.
    b. r is just more than -1.0.
    c. r is just more than 0.0.
    d. r is just less than 1.0.

12. When there is a weak positive relationship
    a. r is just less than 0.0.
    b. r is just more than -1.0.
    c. r is just more than 0.0.
    d. r is just less than 1.0.

13. When there is a strong negative relationship
    a. r is just less than 0.0.
    b. r is just more than -1.0.
    c. r is just more than 0.0.
    d. r is just less than 1.0.

14. When there is a weak negative relationship
    a. r is just less than 0.0.
    b. r is just more than -1.0.
    c. r is just more than 0.0.
    d. r is just less than 1.0.

15. Which of the following reflects a positive correlation?
    a. The ratio of head size to height decreases with age.
    b. Yearly income increases as educational level is increased.
    c. Men own more cars than women.
    d. Amount of exercise is inversely related to rate of heart attacks.

16. The cross-lagged-panel correlation is used to
    a. examine multiple correlations.
    b. partial out irrelevant variables.
    c. examine patterns of correlations over time.
    d. all of the above

17. Subject reactivity is a source of danger in
    a. contingency table research
    b. correlational research
    c. both of the above
    d. neither of the above

18. When we have conducted a proper experiment, we can conclude that the changes in the independent variable were the _____ cause of the change in behavior.
    a. real
    b. ultimate
    c. proximate
    d. all of the above

TRUE- FALSE

____1. In principle, experimental observations permit causal statements.

____2. Pearson's r is often used to analyze contingency tables.

____3. Contingency tables usually are used with nominal data.

____4. Reactivity is not a problem with contingency table research.

____5. Correlation coefficients usually range from 0.0 to 1.0.

___6. Positive values of the correlation coefficient indicate stronger relationships than negative values.

___7. A low correlation between variables A and B is proof that neither variable caused the other.

___8. If an unknown third variable caused both variables A and B, the correlation coefficient would be smaller than if A caused B or vice versa.

___9. Psychology, as all sciences, is concerned with demonstrating ultimate causes for the events in the real world.

ESSAY QUESTIONS

1. Discuss how reactivity is a threat in relational research.
2. Discuss the relationship between causation and correlation.
3. What additional power is provided by a deviant-case study over an ordinary case study? By a cross-lagged-panel correlation procedure over more traditional correlational approaches?

ANSWERS

KEY TERM MATCHING
1. e, a, b, c, d   2. g, c, e, f, a, d

PROGRAMMED REVIEW
1. relational research; (p. 82)
2. contingency tables; (p. 82)
3. cell; (p. 82)
4. frequency; (p. 82)
5. chi square, independence; (p. 83)
6. magnitude, direction; (p. 85)
7. correlation coefficient; (p. 85)
8. predict; (p. 85)
9. -1.0, 1.0; (p. 85)
10. stronger; (p. 85)
11. direction; (p. 85)
12. scatter diagram; (p. 87)
13. causal; (p. 88)

14. third factor; (p. 88)
15. lowered; (p. 90)
16. cross, lagged, panel; (p. 92)
17. experimental; (p. 95)

MULTIPLE CHOICE

1. c; (p. 82)	2. a; (p. 82)	3. d; (p. 82)
4. c; (p. 82)	5. a; (p. 82)	6. d; (p. 82)
7. b; (p. 83)	8. a; (p. 85)	9. a; (p.85)
10. b; (p. 85)	11. d; (p. 85)	12. c; (p. 85)
13. b; (p. 85)	14. a; (p. 85)	15. b; (p. 85)
16. c; (p. 92)	17. c; (p. 92)	18. c; (p. 95)

TRUE- FALSE

1. T; (p. 95)	2. F; (p. 83)	3. T; (p. 82)
4. F; (p. 84)	5. F; (p. 85)	6. F; (p. 85)
7. F; (p. 90)	8. F; (p. 88)	9. F; (p. 95)

CHAPTER 5.

Basics of Experimentation

SUMMARY

I. What is an Experiment?
    A. An experiment is an attempt to arrive at a causal explanation.
    B. John Stuart Mill
        1. argued that causality can be inferred if
            a. a result R follows some event E, and
            b. E and R vary together.
        2. stated that causality can be demonstrated only with the **joint method of agreement and difference**. If E happens, R occurs; if E doesn't happen, neither does R.
    C. The hallmark of an experiment is the production of a *comparison* by controlling the occurrence of an event, holding other aspects *constant*, and observing the outcome that was *produced*.
II. Characteristics of Experimentation
    A. The **experimental group** of subjects receives the important level of the independent variable
    B. The **control group** of subjects receives a comparison level of the independent variable.
    C. Experiments are often more ethical, more economical, and better controlled than alternative research procedures.
III. Variables in Experimentation
    A. Independent Variables
        1. **Independent variables** are those manipulated by the experimenter.
        2. **Null results** - no demonstrated effect - may be obtained if inappropriate levels of the independent variable are selected.

B.   Dependent Variables
1.   **Dependent variables** are what the experimenter measures.
2.   Good dependent variables
a.   are reliable
b.   are sensitive to differences in performance and have an appropriate range of values in the experimental context.
(1)   a **floor effect** is obtained when performance clusters at the low end of the range of possible scores.
(2)   a **ceiling effect** occurs when many scores fall near the upper end of the range.
(3)   Sensitive dependent variables decrease the probability of obtaining null results in an experiment, or committing a **type 2 error** (failing to reject a false null hypothesis of no difference) when statistically analyzing the data.
C.   Control Variables
1.   **Control variables** are potential independent variables that are held constant in an experiment.
2.   Failure to control these variables leads to **confounding**, and makes the proper interpretation of the experimental results difficult or impossible.
D.   Most experiments include more than one independent variable
1.   Combining variables is more efficient than doing several experiments.
2.   Combining variables often offers better experimental control.
3.   The value of the results is increased when they can be shown to occur in many conditions
4.   Psychologically interesting **interactions** occur when the effects of one independent variable are not the same across all levels of another independent variable.
E.   Many experiments include more than one dependent variable for reasons of economy, sensitivity, and to increase the generality of the results.
IV.   Reactivity as a Possible Source of Experimental Error
A.   Experimental subjects have expectations about the nature of the experiment, and these expectations may modify their behavior.
B.   the **Hawthorne effect** is a classic example of the effect on behavior of being observed; work productivity increased throughout the study regardless of the experimental manipulations.
C.   Social roles have been identified   that might influence behavior in a social setting:

1. a person with a **good-subject role** will do anything necessary to validate the experimental hypothesis.
2. a person with a **faithful-subject role** will attempt to be honest and faithful.
3. a person with a **negativistic-subject role** will attempt to sabotage the experiment.
4. a person with an **apprehensive-subject role** is uncomfortable about being evaluated in an experiment. The **evaluation apprehension** leads to responding in a socially desirable way.

D. Attempts to counter the effects of reactivity include
    1. doing **field research** , i.e. using unobtrusive measures in a natural setting
    2. using **deception** to misdirect the subject as to the real purpose of the experiment
    3. withholding from the subject pertinent information about the study.
    4. conducting **simulated experiments** in which subjects are ask to behave as if they were treated in a particular way.

V. External Validity of the Research Procedure
    A. **Subject Representativeness**
        1. refers to whether it is reasonable to generalize from the tested subjects to the population of interest, i.e. whether the same psychological processes involved.
        2. **Reversibility** is a difficulty in establishing subject representativeness. For example disrupting a particular behavior by destroying a brain structure in one species does not necessarily mean that this structure controls the behavior in another species.
        3. It is a good idea to replicate research on members of the population of interest before applying basic research results to practical problems.
    B. **Variable Representativeness**
        1. refers to the extent to which we can generalize from the particular independent variables and their levels actually used in a study.
        2. Variable representativeness can be established by replication employing different experimental manipulations.
    C. **Setting Representativeness**
        1. refers to whether the testing situation has **ecological validity**, and whether the results can be generalized to the real world

2. An important issue is whether the same psychological processes are involved in the research setting as in the real world: if they are, the study has the property of **generalizability**, which is more important than the degree of **realism** of the research setting. Surface realism does not guarantee ecological validity, and ecologically valid results may be obtained in artificial settings.
3. Establishing generalizability is done by replicating research in natural settings.

KEY TERM MATCHING

1.

___apprehensive-subject role

___faithful-subject role

___good-subject role

___negativistic-subject role

a. suffers from evaluation apprehension
b. tries to be honest and faithful
c. tries to mess up the research
d. tries to validate the experimental hypothesis

2.

___ceiling effect

___ex post facto

___floor effect

___Hawthorne effect

___null results

a. classic example of participant reactivity
b. finding no effect of manipulating the independent variable
c. scores are clustered an the upper end of the scale
d. scores are clustered at the lower end of the scale
e. participants are grouped according to some characteristic not produced by the researcher

3.

___confounding

___interaction

___reversibility

___type 2 error

a. a problem in establishing participant representativeness
b. failing to detect an actual treatment effect
c. when something unintended changes along with the experimental manipulation
d. when the effect of one independent variable depends on the level of a second independent variable

4.

___control

___control group

___control variable

___dependent variable

___experimental group

___independent variable

a. participants providing a comparison for the experimental treatment
b. participants receiving the level of interest of the independent variable
c. the essence of experimentation
d. what the experimenter holds constant
e. what the experimenter manipulates
f. what the experimenter measures

5.

___deception

___experiment

___field research

___simulated experiment

a. an application of the joint method of agreement and difference
b. research conducted in a natural setting
c. study in which the participants pretend that they are receiving the experimental treatment
d. when the participants do not know the actual purpose of the study

6.

___generalizability

___realism

___subject representativeness

___setting representativeness

___variable representativeness

a. ecological validity
b. the appearance of naturalness of a research setting
c. the extent to which experimental results can be said to be true
d. the extent to which the independent variables and their levels represent conditions of interest in the real world
e. the extent to which the participants tested represent the people in the population

PROGRAMMED REVIEW

1. The experiment of Brennen et al. was designed to determine whether a _____ or _____ was more important in relieving the tip-of-the-tongue state.

2. An experiment (such as Brennen's study) is designed to allow the researcher to find the _____ of a behavioral event.

3. The method of observation that asserts that "Result R always follows Event E, if E and R vary together and Event E produces Result R" is known as the

_____.

4. One way that control is used in experimentation is that there is a control condition (or group) for purposes of _____.

5. Another form of control in experiments is that we can produce different levels of the _____ variables.

6. A final kind of experimental control is that we can control the _____ _____ and keep these factors constant.

7. The variable that is manipulated or varied is the _____ variable;

8. The events or behaviors that are observed and measured are the _____ variables;

9. Those aspects of the experiment that the researcher holds constant are called the _____ variables.

10. Those participants that receive the level of interest of the independent variable are referred to collectively as the _____ group.

11. The control group is comprised of participants who do not receive the important level of the _____ variable.

12. The major drawback in an ex post facto research project is that the researcher loses experimental _____.

13. When we select an independent variable we do so because we believe it will _____ behavior.

14. A failure of the independent variable to control behavior is sometimes referred to as a _____ _____.

15. If an independent variable is not an important factor in affecting behavior, then an experiment that employs this variable may produce _____ _____.

16. A failure to produce a strong manipulation of the _____ variable may lead to null results.

17. In order for a dependent variable to be useful it is important that the variable produces _____ data.

18. An unreliable dependent variable can often produce _____ results.

19. If performance levels (as measured by the dependent variable) are at the bottom of the measurement scale then this can result in a _____ effect. If performance levels are at the top of the scale then this can result in a _____ effect.

20. It is especially important to control extraneous factors when the magnitude of the effect produced by the independent variable is relatively _____.

21. The most direct experimental technique for controlling extraneous variation is to hold the variable(s) _____.

22. The likelihood of committing a Type 2 error (increases/decreases) _____ as we increase the sensitivity of the dependent variable.

23. It is (more/less) _____ efficient to conduct an experiment with three independent variables than to conduct three separate experiments.

24. If the same results are obtained across several independent variables than these results are said to be _____.

25. If the effects produced by one independent variable are not the same across the levels of a second independent variable this result is termed a(n) _____.

26. Piliavin, Piliavin, and Rodin (1975) conducted an experiment to discover when a bystander would help in an emergency. The independent variables were:
(a)_____ and
(b)_____

27. In an experiment employing only one independent variable it is not possible to obtain _____ effects.

28. In an experiment employing more than one dependent variable the results must be analyzed using _____ statistical procedures.

29. Typically only _____ or _____ dependent variables are used in a single experiment.

30. A well known example of participant reaction is the _____ _____, named after a study in which industrial workers participated in a long experiment.

31. The Hawthorne effect represents one kind of _____.

32. A participant who adopts a _____ _____ role will do anything necessary to validate the experimental hypothesis.

33. Experiments conducted in natural settings are known as _____.

34. Experiments conducted in natural settings suffer from the fact that the _____ that is characteristic of laboratory experiments may be lost in the natural environment.

35. _____ occurs when pertinent information is withheld from the participant.

36. The ability to generalize across different experimental manipulations is called

_____ _____.

37. _____ refers to whether the experimental setting bears a resemblance to the real world.

38. _____ is more important than _____ with respect to setting representativeness.

39. To test the generalizability of experimental results we might repeat the observations in a _____ _____.

40. Concern with ecological validity should be with the psychological _____ being studied.

EXPERIMENTAL PROJECT

As part of a project in an environmental psychology class you are given the following assignment: Determine whether it is possible to "defend" a table in the library by preventing anyone else from sitting down at the table with you.

How would you conduct an experiment to answer this question? What is the hypothesis you want to test? After you have formulated a testable hypothesis, design an experiment to test this hypothesis, then identify the independent, dependent, and control variables.

Now that you have designed your experiment you might want to actually conduct the experiment. However, check with your instructor before you run off to the library: most colleges and universities have regulations concerning research involving human participants. There may be ethical reasons why you can not or should not perform your experiment. (See Chapter 3 for a discussion of ethics in psychological research.)

EXPERIMENTAL DILEMMA

Male college students are recruited to participate in a motor learning experiment. The task being used required the subjects to throw a dart at a one inch diameter target mounted on a wall 10 feet from the subject. The researcher was interested in the effects of monetary incentives on learning this task. All subjects were first given 10 practice throws before the experiment began. Subjects in the high-incentive group were told they would receive 10 cents for every successful throw. Subjects in the low-incentive group were offered 5 cents for each successful throw. Subjects in both groups were also told that they would receive $3.50 just for participating in the experiment, in addition to the payments for successful throws.

Subjects were assigned to the two groups at random. All subjects were given 50 throws. The results showed that there was no significant difference between the two groups in terms of the number of successful throws. The researcher concluded that monetary incentives have no effect on performance in this type of task.

Would you accept this conclusion? Are there any additional data that would allow you to answer this question more confidently?

MULTIPLE CHOICE

1. In Brennen's experiments on the tip-of-the-tongue (TOT) state, the independent variable was _____ and the dependent variable was _____.
   a. the cuing condition; percent of pictures identified
   b. the cuing condition; percent of TOTs resolved
   c. sex of the celebrity; percent of pictures identified
   d. sex of the celebrity; percent of TOTs resolved

2. We can use John Stuart Mills joint method of agreement and difference to decide that cuing with initials caused an increase in TOT resolutions because
   a. with initials there was increased resolution.
   b. without initials there was no increased resolution.
   c. both a and b
   d. neither a nor b

3. The hallmark of an experiment is
   a. repeated positive correlations.
   b. repeated significant effects.
   c. producing a comparison by controlling the occurrence/nonoccurrence of a variable and observing the outcome.
   d. random assignment of subjects to conditions and tight procedural control over variables.

4. If two variables occur together in nature, then there is no control over the presumed cause. As a result this observation reveals:
   a. correlations.
   b. causal relations.
   c. descriptive data.
   d. unreliable data.
   e. only strong relations.

5. In an experiment, the variable manipulated by the experimenter is the _____ variable and the behavior recorded by the experimenter is the _____ variable.
   a. independent; dependent
   b. dependent; independent
   c. observed; control
   d. control; observed

6. Dependent variables are dependent upon
   a. experimental manipulations.
   b. behavior of the subject.
   c. experimental control.
   d. comparisons produced experimentally.
   e. being held constant.

7. The variable manipulated by the experimenter in order to study its effect on behavior is called the
   a. control variable.
   b. experimental variable.
   c. dependent variable.
   d. independent variable.

8. In principle, experiments are designed to allow the researcher to make statements about
    a. causation.
    b. contiguity.
    c. correlation.
    d. strength of relations.
    e. both b and c

9. Null results can be caused by problems associated with the _____ variable(s).
    a. control
    b. experimental
    c. independent
    d. dependent
    e. both c and d

10. A good dependent variable should be
    a. reliable.
    b. related to the independent variable.
    c. of theoretical interest.
    d. easy to observe.

11. Floor effects and ceiling effects result from using
    a. an unreliable dependent variable.
    b. only one level of the independent variable.
    c. two very extreme levels of the independent variable.
    d. a restricted range of the dependent variable.

12. A control variable is
    a. a potential dependent variable that is held constant.
    b. a potential independent variable that is held constant.
    c. a dependent variable that is varied in a controlled fashion by the experimenter.
    d. an independent variable that is varied in a controlled fashion by the experimenter.

13. Which of the following is not an advantage of manipulating several independent variables within the same experiment, as opposed to manipulating these variables in separate experiments?
    a. greater efficiency
    b. interaction effects may be observed
    c. control variables are more likely to be held constant
    d. results are easier to interpret

14. Which of the following is not one of the ways that control is used in an experiment?
    a. The control group is used as a basis of comparison.
    b. The independent variable is under controlled manipulation.
    c. The independent variable is directly controlled by the researcher.
    d. Extraneous variables are controlled by being held constant.
    e. All of the above represent ways in which control is used.

15. The "control" in control variable refers to
    a. the influence exerted on behavior.
    b. the fact that the experimenter must control the variable to ensure a valid comparison.
    c. the fact that the control group experiences the variable.
    d. the fact that the variable is subject to controlled manipulation in the experiment.
    e. the fact that the variable is under the direct control of the subject.

16. An interaction occurs when
    a. the effects produced by one independent variable are not the same at each level of a second independent variable.
    b. the effects produced by one level of an independent variable are not the same at other levels of that independent variable.
    c. the effects produced by an independent variable are not the same at each level of the dependent variable.
    d. the effects produced by a dependent variable are not the same at each level of the independent variable.

17. A valid experiment may produce null results because:
    a. the levels of the independent variable are too similar to each other.
    b. the dependent variable is subject to a ceiling effect.
    c. extraneous variables are not held constant.
    d. all of the above
    e. both a and b

18. Which of the following fictional results is not an example of an interaction?
    a.   with normally active children, the stimulating effect of amphetamines increases as the dosage increases, but with hyperactive children the greater the dosage of amphetamines, the calmer the children
    b.   the level of humidity greatly affects people's comfort levels in the summer heat, but in the winter cold humidity levels make much less of a difference on comfort levels
    c.   people who attend church regularly donate more money to charity than nonchurchgoers unless they are poor, in which case church attendance makes no difference
    d.   children who watch violent TV shows are more aggressive than children who do not watch violent TV shows, although all children watch the same amount of TV
    e.   college men go out drinking more often than college women, unless they are poor, in which case women go out drinking more often

19. The nature of the interaction in the study by Piliavin, Piliavin and Rodin was
    a.   presence or absence of the intern had little effect if the victim had no birthmark but a large effect if the victim had a birthmark.
    b.   presence or absence of an intern was more important than presence or absence of a birthmark.
    c.   presence or absence of a birthmark was more important than presence or absence of an intern.
    d.   the presence or absence of a birthmark had a larger effect when the intern was present than when the intern was not present.
    e.   both a and b

20. The Hawthorne Effect is a classic example of
    a.   participant reaction in an experiment.
    b.   experimenter bias.
    c.   field research using unobtrusive measures.
    d.   mistakenly inferring causation from a correlation.

21. The Orne and Evans (1965) study involving asking subjects to perform dangerous acts demonstrates
    a.   social conformity.
    b.   a lack of ecological validity.
    c.   unethical research.
    d.   the volunteer problem.
    e.   demand characteristics.

22. Which of the following is not a social role described by Weber and Cook (1972)?
    a. apprehensive-subject role
    b. faithful-subject
    c. good-subject role
    d. negativistic-subject role
    e. none of the above

23. In a simulated experiment
    a. the demands of the situation are assumed to be the same for participants in all conditions.
    b. a laboratory experiment is replicated in an environment created to simulate the real world.
    c. there is greater ecological validity than in a laboratory experiment.
    d. both b and c

24. Ecological validity refers to the ability to generalize research finds to the _____ to which they are intended to apply.
    a. population
    b. people
    c. species
    d. environmental settings
    e. both b and d

25. Ecological validity is
    a. more dependent on generalizability than on surface realism.
    b. more dependent on surface realism than on generalizability.
    c. equally dependent on surface realism and generalizability.
    d. does not depend on either surface realism or on generalizability.

TRUE-FALSE

____1. Graessle et al found that rats given prenatal decompressions began to climb at a later age, and gained weight more slowly than controls.

____2. The joint method of agreement and difference asserts that if a series of observations all agree on a specific ordering of two events than the first event must have caused the second event.

____3. The joint method of agreement and difference requires pairs of observations made at the same time by the different observers.

___4. The sole difference between the experimental group and the control group is that the former receives the independent variable whereas the later does not receive this variable.

___5. Ex post facto research involves examining the aftereffects of the experimental manipulation employed by the researcher.

___6. Null results generally only have one interaction.

___7. An important criterion for a good dependent variable is reliability.

___8. When the dependent variable is restricted to a narrow range near the top of the scale of measurement this indicates a ceiling effect.

___9. Experimental control is usually better in three experiments each employing one independent variable than it is in a single experiment employing three independent variables.

___10. An interaction is obtained when the effect produced by one independent variable is not the same at different levels of another independent variable.

___11. Whenever interaction effects are obtained it does not make sense to consider separately the effects of each independent variable involved in the interaction.

___12. The Hawthorne Effect is a classic example of participant reactivity.

___13. Field experiments maintain a higher level of control than is possible in a laboratory experiment.

___14. If the results of a simulated experiment are highly similar to the results obtained with the independent variable, we can concluded that the independent variable effectively controls behavior.

___15. Results concerning the operation of sensory processes in college students is very likely to generalize to other people.

ESSAY QUESTIONS

1. Define the three types of variables involved in an experiment, giving an example of each type of variable.

2. What are null results? What are the reasons why an otherwise valid experiment might produce null results?

3.   What is an interaction? How do interactions affect the way in which the results of an experiment are interpreted?

4.   What is ecological validity? How can a researcher increase the ecological validity of his studies?

ANSWERS

KEY TERM MATCHING

1. a, b, d, c
2. c, d, e, a, b
3. c, d, a, b
4. c, a, d, f, b, e
5. d, a, b, c
6. c. b, e, a, d

PROGRAMMED REVIEW

1. picture, initials; (p. 101)
2. cause; (p. 102)
3. joint method of agreement and difference; (p. 103)
4. comparison; (p. 106)
5. independent; (p. 106)
6. environmental factors; (p. 106)
7. independent; (p. 107)
8. dependent; (p. 108)
9. control; (p. 109)
10. experimental; (p. 106)
11. independent; (p. 106)
12. control; (p. 106)
13. affect; (p. 107)
14. null result; (p. 108)
15. null results; (p. 108)
16. independent; (p. 108)
17. reliable; (p. 108)
18. null results; (p. 109)
19. floor, ceiling; (p. 109)
20. small; (p. 109)
21. constant; (p. 109)
22. decrease; (p. 109)
23. more; (p. 112)
24. generalizable; (p. 113)
25. interaction; (p. 115)
26. presence and absence of birthmark, presence and absence of intern; (p. 113)
27. interaction; (p. 113)
28. multivariate; (p. 116)

29. one, two; (p. 116)
30. Hawthorne effect; (p. 118)
31. reactivity; (p. 118)
32. good subject; (p. 119)
33. field research; (p. 125)
34. control; (p. 125)
35. deception; (p. 121)
36. variable representativeness; (p. 124)
37. realism; (p. 125)
38. generalizability, realism; (p. 125)
39. natural setting; (p. 125)
40. process; (p. 125)

MULTIPLE CHOICE

1. b; (p. 101)
2. c; (p. 103)
3. c; (p. 104)

4. a; (p. 104)
5. a; (p. 106)
6. a; (p. 108)

7. d; (p. 107)
8. a; (p. 108)
9. e; (p. 108, 109)

10. a; (p. 108)
11. d; (p. 109)
12. b; (p. 109)

13. d; (p. 112)
14. e; (p. 110)
15. b; (p. 109)

16. a; (p. 114)
17. d; (p. 108, 109, 110)
18. d; (p. 113)

19. d; (p. 114)
20. a; (p. 118)
21. e; (p. 119)

22. e; (p. 120)
23. a; (p. 122)
24. d; (p. 125)

25. a; (p. 125)

TRUE-FALSE

1. T; (p. 106)   2. F; (p. 103)   3. F; (p. 103)

4. F; (p. 108)   5. F; (p. 107)   6. F; (p. 108)

7. T; (p. 108)   8. T; (p. 109)   9. F; (p. 113)

10. T; (p. 113)   11. T; (p. 115)   12. T; (p. 118)

13. F; (p. 125)   14. F; (p. 122)   15. T; (p. 123)

CHAPTER 6.

Conducting Ethical Research

SUMMARY

I.   Research with human participants
     A.   Responsible psychologists follow the ethical guidelines provided by the American Psychological Association, including
          1.   Evaluating the ethical acceptability of proposed research
          2.   Determining whether a participant is a "subject at risk" or a "subject at minimal risk"
          3.   Retaining the responsibility for ensuring ethical practices
          4.   Obtaining **informed consent** from research participants
          5.   Using deception only when the benefits of the research outweigh any risks to the participants
          6.   Respecting an individual's freedom to refuse to participate in the research and the participant's **freedom to withdraw** from the research at any time
          7.   Ensuring that the participants are **protected from harm**
          8.   **Debriefing** the participants as soon as possible
          9.   **Removing harmful consequences** to the participant
          10. Maintaining the participant's **confidentiality**
II. Ethics in Research with Animals
     A.   Animals are used in research because
          1.   It would be difficult or impractical to answer certain questions with human participants
          2.   Animals are interesting in their own right
          3.   Animals provide convenient, highly controlled models for humans and for other animals
     B.   Arguments for and against research with animals include

        1.   Animals feel pain and their lives can be destroyed, as is true of humans
            a.   but, ethical animal research is conducted only when the benefits exceed any harm to the animals
        2.   Destroying any living thing is dehumanizing to the scientist
            a.   but, a majority of animal-rights activists eat meat, and or purchase leather goods
        3.   Using animals in research is a form of prejudice called **speciesism** and as such, is completely unethical
            a.   but, much animal research benefits other animals
            b.   few people would be willing to give up the benefits that derive from animal research including advances in neurosurgery and understanding and treatment of many psychological disorders

   C.   Guidelines for use of animals in research include
        1.   Acquisition, care, use, and disposal of all animals in compliance with the law
        2.   Supervision by a trained psychologist of all procedures involving animals
        3.   Minimizing pain, discomfort, and illness of animals
        4.   Terminating an animal's life rapidly and painlessly

III.   Scientific Fraud
   A.   Cases of deliberate research bias include
        1.   Sir Cyril Burt's work on heredity and intelligence
        2.   The Piltdown Man
   B.   Fraud will eventually be discovered through **replication** of research

IV.   Monitoring Ethical Practices
   A.   The American Psychological Association established an Ethics Committee which
        1.   Educates the public and psychologists
        2.   Investigates complaints about unethical research practices
   B.   **Institutional Review Boards**
        1.   Required by institutions receiving federal funds for research
        2.   Approve proposed research at these institutions

KEY TERM MATCHING

1.

___ aftercare

___ confidentiality

___ debriefing

___ deception

___ fraud

___ freedom to withdraw

___ informed consent

___ institutional review board

___ protection from harm

___ removing harmful consequences

___ replication

___ speciesism

a. a committee that monitors ethical practices at an institution

b. allowing a participant to call a halt to his continued participation in an experiment

c. deliberate misrepresentation of research results

d. ensuring that a participant is in as good physical and mental shape at the end of an experiment as he is at the beginning

e. explaining to a participant the purpose of an experiment at its conclusion

f. given by the participant before participation in a study

g. a manipulation to reduce reactivity

h. not talking about the experimental performance of individual participants

i. prejudice against lower animals

j. process by which science is self-correcting

k. responsibility for possibly long-term effects

l. the overriding ethical principle

PROGRAMMED REVIEW

1. Most universities and research institutions have _____ committees that judge the ethicality of proposed research.

2. Individuals should read and understand the ethical principles of the American Psychological Association _____ they conduct a research project with human participants.

3. Participants should be warned ahead of time if there is any potential _____ _____ that might result from participating in the experiment.

4. The experimenter is obliged to _____ participants of any potential harm. .

5. Psychologists who conduct research with human participants are obliged to respect the _____ and _____ of the participants in the research.

6. Individuals must be given the option of _____ from the research at any time.

7. Deception is sometimes used to control participant _____ .

8. When students taking an introductory psychology course are required to participate in experiments as part of a course requirement, they should have some _____ way of fulfilling this requirement.

9. _____ means that the experimenter explains the general purposes of the research and the nature of the manipulations used.

10. Unless otherwise agreed, what a subject does in an experiment should be _____ .

11. Ethical decisions are rarely made on the basis of _____ facts.

12. _____ is a form of racism involving claims about scientific progress being helped by animal research.

13. Animal subjects should be treated humanely, and the decision to inflict pain on an animal should be based on a weighing of the _____ and _____ of the research.

14. As a model for _____ and _____ behavior, animal research is essential for scientific progress.

15. _____ is intentional researcher bias. It can be detected when other researchers fail to _____ the original results.

EXPERIMENTAL PROJECT

This project is designed to get you to consider in more detail the issues of ethics in research. Make up a short list of experiments that you think are in some way unethical, but that you might like to perform just to see what happens. Visit faculty members who specialize in the research areas of your experiments and ask them if they would be willing to supervise the experiments.

Did the faculty members question the ethics of your proposed experiment? How many faculty members told you that they refuse because the proposed research is unethical? How many tried to see if there might be a way to answer the question posed in your research, but using an ethical experiment? Finally, after reading the issues raised in the chapter, would you consider this to be an ethical project? Why or why not?

EXPERIMENTAL DILEMMA

A social psychologist is interested in studying how decisions are made concerning ethics in research by peer evaluation committees. In other words, she wants to study the university committee that decides whether or not a proposed research project conforms to conventional ethical standards. The problem confronted by this research is that she needs to get the approval of this committee before she can study them.

Is it possible to conduct internally and externally valid research on this issue? What ethical problems might the research face? How could she avoid demand characteristics, or reactivity, from affecting her results? Assume for the moment that one of the ways this psychologist intends to study the decision-making process is to submit fake research proposals under the name of another (consenting) researcher. Some of these proposals would violate ethical standards, others would not. Is this an ethical approach? How might you design a research project to address the problem of interest (i.e., the decision-making process)?

MULTIPLE CHOICE

1. The principle of informed consent means that the researcher has an obligation to
    a. submit all research proposals to a peer committee that will judge the ethics of the proposed research.
    b. tell subjects prior to participation all aspects of the research that might reasonably be expected to influence willingness to participate.
    c. only disclose the results of the experiment after he has obtained the consent of all subjects who participated in the study.
    d. agree to perform the research only after he or she is certain that no ethical standards are being violated.

2. In an ethical research project
    a. informed consent is obtained from all participants.
    b. participants may withdraw at any time.
    c. the potential gains outweigh the potential harm.
    d. all of the above
    e. both a and b

3. In the Elmes, et al study on depression and memory
    a. the researchers did not deceive the participants.
    b. both the experimental and control group received depression induction.
    c. subjects in the control group responded as if they were depressed.
    d. participants were given a list of people to contact if the depression continued.

4. One problem associated with providing enough information for informed consent is that
    a. the validity of the experimental design may be undermined.
    b. people may avoid participating in all psychology research, even low-risk studies.
    c. some research projects may not be able to obtain subjects.
    d. it is a time-consuming process.

5. Debriefing means that
    a. the investigator is aware of the potential risks involved is the experiment.
    b. the investigator explains the general purpose of the research after the study is completed.
    c. the investigator provides the ethics committee with an abstract of each proposed research project.
    d. after a blind experiment is run the investigator tells the research assistants what the purpose of the experiment was.

6. Animals are often used as subjects in psychological research because
   a. ethical considerations are generally less stringent with animal research than with human research.
   b. they are interesting.
   c. they form an important part of the natural world.
   d. all of the above
   e. both b and c

7. Singer (1978) calls claims about scientific progress being helped by animal research
   a. anthropomorphism.
   b. explicitly unethical.
   c. speciesism.
   d. unfounded.
   e. all of the above

TRUE-FALSE

____1. Any federally funded research must be approved by an ethics review committee before any funding is granted.

____2. In a research project, every member of the research team is responsible for ensuring ethical practice in research.

____3. In the Elmes, et al (1984) study on the effect of depression on memory, subjects were told about the possible side effects of the depressant drug during the debriefing session.

____4. Providing information for informed consent generally helps reduce the reactivity of the experimental design.

____5. Participants are always allowed to withdraw from an experiment regardless of their reasons for withdrawing.

____6. Informed consent is generally obtained in writing during the debriefing session.

____7. Confidentiality means that, in general, results of an experiment are not published unless the subject gives his or her approval.

____8. Ethical decisions are never made on the basis of pragmatic concerns.

ESSAY QUESTIONS

1. Under what circumstances (if any) might an ethics review committee allow an experiment involving deception to be conducted?

2. Describe in your own words the argument used in the textbook to argue in favor of animal research.

3. What is meant by aftercare? How would this concept relate to the famous Milgram studies on obedience in which participants though they were giving electric shocks to another person?

ANSWERS

KEY TERM MATCHING

1. k, h, e, g, c, b, f, a, l, d, j, i

PROGRAMMED REVIEW

1. peer; (p. 134)
2. before; (p. 135)
3. detrimental effects; (p. 137)
4. inform; (p. 136)
5. dignity, welfare; (p. 135)
6. withdrawing; (p. 136)
7. reactivity; (p. 137)
8. optional; (p. 139)
9. debriefing; (p. 139)
10. confidential; (p. 140)
11. objective; (p. 141)
12. speciesism; (p. 144)
13. costs, benefits; (p. 145)
14. human, animal; (p. 144)
15. fraud, replicate; (p. 150)

MULTIPLE CHOICE

1. b; (p. 137)	2. d; (p. 141)	3. d; (p. 139)
4. a; (p. 137)	5. b; (p. 139)	6. a; (p. 143)
7. b; (p. 143)		

TRUE-FALSE

1. T; (p. 134)	2. T; (p. 135)	3. F; (p. 139)
4. F; (p. 137)	5. T; (p. 138)	6. F; (p. 137)
7. F; (p. 140)	8. F; (p. 141)	

CHAPTER 7

Exploring the Literature of Psychology

SUMMARY

I.   Literature Searches
   A.   are useful to find out
      1.   if others have already done your proposed experiment
      2.   "tricks of the trade" that may be useful in designing an experiment
   B.   Useful general resources include
      1.   **Psychological Abstracts** which contains brief abstract of articles from most journals that publish psychological research
      2.   **Computerized literature searches** are very efficient in generating a list of appropriate articles
      3.   **Social Science Citation Index** lists recent articles that reference a critical article

II. Parts of an Article
   A.   **Title** and **Author**(s)
      1.   Titles often state the independent and dependent variables
      2.   Familiar authors often identify articles of interest
   B.   **Abstract** - a concise summary of the article
   C.   **Introduction**
      1.   Specifies problem to be studied
      2.   Reviews relevant literature
      3.   Specifies the research hypothesis
   D.   **Method**
      1.   Contains enough information to allow replication of the study
      2.   Usually divided into subsections:
         a.   **Participants** - how many, how selected, who they were

        b.   **Apparatus** or **Materials** - equipment or questionnaires, etc. used to test the subjects

        c.   **Procedure** - explains what happened to the subjects

E.   **Results**

    1.   Summarized data

        a.   Descriptive statistics

        b.   **Tables**

        c.   **Figures** are graphs that plot the

           (1)   dependent variable on the Y axis or **ordinate**

           (2)   independent variable on the X axis or **abscissa**

    2.   Inferential statistics are used to determine how sure we can be that any differences between treatment conditions are not due to chance

F.   **Discussion** - an interpretation of the results

G.   **References** - bibliographic citations for articles referenced in the current study

III. Checklist for the Critical Reader

   A.   After reading the **introduction**, you should know

      1.   the author's goal

      2.   what hypothesis is tested

      3.   how *you* would test this hypothesis

   B.   After reading the **method**, you should

      1.   consider whether your proposed method is better than the author's

      2.   consider whether the author's method actually tests the hypothesis

      3.   identify the dependent, independent, and control variables

      4.   predict what you think will happen in the experiment

   C.   After reading the **results**, you should decide

      1.   whether the results were unexpected

      2.   how you would interpret the obtained results

      3.   what applications and implications would you draw from your interpretation

   D.   After reading the **discussion**, you should decide

      1.   whether your interpretation or the author's best represents the data

      2.   whether you or the author offers the most cogent discussion of the applications and implications of the results

KEY TERM MATCHING

1.

____ abscissa
____ figure
____ ordinate
____ PsychINFO
____ *Psychological Abstracts*
____ references
____ *Social Science Citation Index*
____ tables

a. citations of articles referred to in present article
b. computerized psychological data base
c. collection of summaries of research articles
d. graph of summarized data
e. lists recent articles that reference a target article
f. non-graphical data summary
g. where dependent variable is plotted
h. where independent variable is plotted

2.

____ apparatus
____ author
____ abstract
____ discussion
____ introduction
____ materials
____ method
____ participants
____ procedure
____ results
____ title

a. appears after the title on the first page
b. describes equipment used in study
c. where inferential statistics are used
d. names independent and dependent variables
e. presents enough information for study to be replicated
f. summary of the key points of article
g. what happens to the participant
h. where a questionnaire would be presented
i. where problem is presented
j. where results are interpreted
k. where selection of participants is described

PROGRAMMED REVIEW

1. The seven parts of a basic psychology article are a)_____ and _____, b)_____, c)_____, d)_____, e)_____, f)_____, and g)_____

2. Most titles state the _____ and _____ variables.

3. The _____ is a short paragraph that summarizes the key points of the article.

4. The references are found at the _____ of an article.

5. The Introduction should specify the _____ to be studied, the _____ to be tested and the rationale behind any _____.

6. If you wanted to replicate an experiment you would need to consult the _____ section in the article that describes the experiment

7. The Method section is sometimes divided up into three subsections that cover: _____, _____, and _____.

8. The _____ section contains a summary of what happened in the experiment.

9. If different figures are included in an article it is important to check that the _____ are comparable so that effects can be compared across figures.

10. Extra skepticism (on the part of the reader) is required when reading the _____ section.

11. Before you read the Method section you should try to design an _____ to test the _____ stated in the Introduction.

12. After you have read the Method section you should check to see that the methods used are adequate for testing the _____.

13. You should try to predict the results for the experiment before reading the _____ section.

14. Any published reports cited in a paper are listed in the _____.

EXPERIMENTAL PROJECT

The best way to get good at reading journal articles is through practice. The more articles you read the more proficient you will become at reading reports. Each time you read an article you should try to answer all of the suggested questions for critical readers). For further practice reading journal articles, consult your university library. Research articles in the *Psychonomic Bulletin & Review* are good for practice reading, since there is a page limit for the articles that appear in that journal. Finally, it is a good idea to get together with classmates and decide upon one or more articles to read. After you have read the articles(s) and <u>written out</u> your answers to the questions, you should compare you answers with your classmates.

MULTIPLE CHOICE

1. In which of the following sources would you not generally expect to find review articles?
    a.   American Psychologist
    b.   Journal of Experimental Social Psychology
    c.   Psychological Bulletin
    d.   Psychological Review

2. Perhaps the best place to start in developing a list of references for a problem in psychology that is new to you is:
    a.   American Journal of Psychology.
    b.   The American Psychologist.
    c.   Annual Review of Psychology.
    d.   Psychological Abstracts.
    e.   Social Science Citation Index.

3. A journal that allows you to identify recent articles that have referenced a critical key article is
    a.   Current Contents.
    b.   Annual Review of Psychology.
    c.   Bulletin of the Psychonomic Society.
    d.   Social Science Citation Index.

4. Each of the following is a part of a journal article except the _____.
    a.   introduction
    b.   method
    c.   results
    d.   discussion
    e.   summary

5. In the "Introduction" of a journal article the author should
    a.   specify the problem to be studied.
    b.   specify the hypothesis (or hypotheses) to be tested.
    c.   give the rationale behind any predictions.
    d.   all of the above

6. Which of the following should be included in the "Method" section of a journal article?
   a. considerations concerning subjects
   b. a description of the apparatus used in the experiment
   c. the procedure of the experiment
   d. all of the above
   e. both a and b

7. Which of the following would be unusual to find in the "Results" section of a journal article?
   a. raw data
   b. summary statistics
   c. inferential statistics
   d. the level of significance

8. The interpretation of the experimental findings is found in the _____.
   a. abstract
   b. introduction
   c. method
   d. results
   e. discussion

9. The question "What hypothesis will be tested?" should be answered by reading the _____.
   a. abstract
   b. introduction
   c. method
   d. results
   e. discussion

10. The question "What is the independent variable?" should be answered by reading the _____.
    a. abstract
    b. introduction
    c. method
    d. results
    e. discussion

11. The question "Are the results expected?" should be answered by reading the
_____.
   a. abstract
   b. introduction
   c. method
   d. results
   e. discussion

12. The question "Is my interpretation better than the author's?" should be answered
    by reading the _____.
   a. abstract
   b. introduction
   c. method
   d. results
   e. discussion

TRUE-FALSE

___1. The introduction of a journal article specifies the hypothesis to be studied
       and briefly describes the experiment designed to test the hypothesis.

___2. Statistical design features of an experiment are described in the "Method"
       section of a journal article.

___3. The statement "$F(6,20) = 7.40$, p $= .01$" means that the odds for obtaining
       an F-statistic at least as large as 7.40 by chance if the experiment were
       repeated would be one percent.

___4. In the "Discussion" section of a journal article, the author is free to
       interpret the results, and thus the reader must accept the author's
       interpretation.

___5. The most important question for the reader to answer after reading the
       "Method" section is: Is this how I would design an experiment to test this
       hypothesis?

ESSAY QUESTIONS

1. Name the sections of a journal article and briefly describe the function of each
    section.

2. Why is it important to be wary of statements like "although the improvement observed following training did not quite achieve the level of significance, it is clear that the data reveal a trend in the predicted direction?"

ANSWERS

KEY TERM MATCHING

1. h, d, g, b, c, a, e, f

2. b, a, f, j, i, h, e, k, g, c, d

PROGRAMMED REVIEW

1. a) title, author(s), b) abstract, c) introduction, d) method, e) results, f) discussions, g) references; (p. 159)
2. dependent, independent; (p. 159)
3. abstract; (p. 159)
4. end; (p. 167)
5. problem, hypothesis, predictions; (p. 160)
6. method; (p. 160)
7. participants, apparatus or materials, procedure; (p. 160)
8. results; (p. 160)
9. scale; (p.166)
10. discussion; (p. 167)
11. method, hypothesis; (p. 168)
12. hypothesis; (p. 168)
13. results; (p. 169)
14. references; (p. 167)

MULTIPLE CHOICE

1. b; (p. 157)   2. d; (156)   3. d; (p. 156)

4. e; (p. 159)   5. d; (p. 159)   6. d; (p. 160)

7. a; (p. 160)   8. e; (p. 167)   9. b; (p. 168)

10. c; (p. 169)   11. d; (p. 169)   12. e; (p. 170)

TRUE-FALSE

1. F (p. 159   2. F (p. 160)   3. T (p. 166

4. F (p. 167)   5. F; (p. 169)

CHAPTER 8.

Measurement in Psychological Research

SUMMARY

I. Measurement Scales
   A. **Measurement** is a systematic way of assigning numbers or names to objects or their attributes.
   B. Properties of Measurement Scales
      1. **Difference** - there are instances of measured objects that are different from each other. All measurement scales are sensitive to differences
      2. **Magnitude** - some measurement scales reflect the magnitudes of the measured attribute.
      3. **Equal Intervals** - Some scales have the property of using equally sized units to measure magnitude.
      4. **True Zero** - one measurement scale has the property that value of zero means the complete absence of the attribute being measured.
   C. Types of Measurement Scales
      1. **Nominal scales** measure only the property of differences. Scale values are simply names.
      2. **Ordinal scales** measure differences in magnitude. Measured objects can be ranked from least to most of the measured attribute.
      3. **Interval scales** measure magnitude with equally sized units. Interval measures can be meaningfully added and averaged.
      4. **Ratio scales** have all four of the above properties. Because there is a true zero point, it is meaningful to say that a score that is twice as large as another score represents twice as much of the measured attribute.
   D. Importance of Measurement Scales
      1. Ratio scales provide the most information, and nominal scales provide the least information of any of the scale types.

2. Measurements can be analyzed meaningfully with any statistical methods appropriate for any lesser level, but not for higher levels of measurement.

3. The level of measurement of the data limit the kinds of conclusions that can be drawn from research.

II. Measurement Procedures

   A. **Theoretical Constructs**

      1. Intervening variables are often called theoretical constructs because they tie together several independent (input) and dependent (output) variables.

      2. When the inputs can be specified physically, **psychophysical scaling** can be used to measure the theoretical concept.

      3. When the inputs are less clearly specified, **psychometric scaling** is used to measure the theoretical concept.

   B. Psychophysical Scaling

      1. **Psychophysics** is the study and measurement of psychological reactions to physical events having a known dimension.

      2. Psychophysical Scales

         a. An **absolute threshold** is the least amount of stimulus energy required to detect a stimulus.

         b. A **difference threshold** is the smallest change in stimulus magnitude that can be detected.

         c. Weber discovered that

            (1) the magnitude of the difference threshold increases with the magnitude of the standard stimulus,

            (2) the ratio of the difference threshold (ΔI) to the standard stimulus (I) is constant ($\Delta I/I = K$) within a particular sensory modality. This relationship is known as **Weber's law.**

            (3) Weber's law holds for about 90 percent to the range of standard stimuli, but fails to hold for very weak stimuli.

   C. Psychometric Scaling

      1. Cumulative Scales

         a. **Cumulative scales** are often called **Guttman scales,** since he developed them.

         b. In a perfect cumulative scale, a person with a higher *total* score than another, scores as high, or higher than the other person *on every item on the test.*

    c.   The adequacy of Guttman scales can be measured by the **coefficient of reproducibility**, the ratio of consistent to total responses, which should be at least .9 for an acceptable scale.

    d.   Example of the use of Guttman scales include

        (1)   measurement of participation in union activities

        (2)   measurement of substance use, and determining the consistency of the order of using various substances.

    e.   There is disagreement about the level of measurement provided by a cumulative scale. Many psychometricians believe that the ratio level is achieved, while more conservative estimates suggest the ordinal level.

  2.   Summated Rating Scale

    a.   **Summated rating scales** were developed by Likert, and are also known as **Likert scales**.

    b.   Subjects indicate the extent of their agreement (SA A U D SD) with several statements dealing with the topic being measured.

    c.   Each response alternative is associated with a number

    d.   The subject's score is the sum of the numbers associated with the selected response alternatives.

    e.   Items on a Likert scale are evaluated by determining how well they reflect the total score received by an individual. This relationship is measured by the **coefficient of correlation**.

    f.   Usually Likert scales are believed to measure at the interval level; a more cautious view is that since the total score is actually a sum of rankings, it is more properly regarded as an ordinal measure.

  3.   Self-Report Methods

    a.   Both the cumulative scale and the summated rating scale are examples of **self-report methods**; the data come from personal reports rather than from observations.

    b.   Since the data cannot be corroborated by the observer it is difficult to determine the validity of the measurements.

III. Reliability and Validity of Measurement

  A. **Validity** refers to

    1.   the soundness and meaningfulness of operations

    2.   whether a test actually measures what it is intended to measure

        a.   determined by comparing test scores against a **criterion**

          b.   when test scores correlate well with criterion measures, the test is said to have **predictive validity**

B.   **Reliability** refers to

    1.   consistency of measurement

    2.   Reliability of a measure

        a.   **test-retest reliability** involves correlating the scores obtained from two administrations of a test to the same people to determine if the measurement procedure is stabile over time.

        b.   **parallel forms** reliability involves correlating the scores from two different versions of the same test to determine whether both forms measure the same thing.

        c.   **split-half reliability** involves correlating the scores made on one half of a test with the scored made on the other half of the test. A high correlation indicates that different parts of the test are measuring the same attribute.

    3.   **Statistical reliability** is determined by the use of inferential statistics which indicate the probability of obtaining a set of results by chance. If this probability is sufficiently low, the results are said to be statistically reliable.

IV. Sampling

    A.   Most research is performed on a **sample**, or subset of the **population** of interest.

    B.   Increasing the size of this sample increases the **power** of statistical tests, their ability to identify non-chance effects of independent variables.

    C.   **Random sampling** from the population, when each member of the population has an equal chance of being included in the sample, increases the chances that the sample will be representative of the population, especially when the sample is large.

    D.   When the sample represents the population, the conclusions of a study are said to be **externally valid** and are applicable to the population as a whole.

    E.   **Internal validity** refers to the extent that we can be sure that experimental results were due to the manipulation of the independent variable, and not to some confounding influence. Random assignment of subjects to treatment conditions reduces the likelihood of confounding arising from subject differences, and thereby increases the internal validity.

    F.   **Experimental Reliability** is high when the same results are obtained when a study is replicated.

KEY TERM MATCHING

1.

____ absolute threshold

____ difference threshold

____ just-noticeable difference

    a.   minimum stimulus intensity necessary for detection

    b.   minimum detectable change in stimulus intensity

    c.   psychological response to a barely detectable change in stimulus intensity

2.

____ coefficient of correlation

____ coefficient of reproducibility

____ criterion

____ power

    a.   ability of a statistical test to detect treatment effects in an experiment

    b.   another and trusted measure of a psychometrically measured attribute

    c.   measurement of the degree of relationship between two variables

    d.   used to determine the adequacy of Guttman scales

3.

____ nominal

____ interval

____ ordinal

____ ratio

    a.   measures differences and magnitude only

    b.   measures differences only

    c.   units of measurement are the same size for any stimulus magnitude

    d.   zero point means the absence of the measured attribute

4.

____ cumulative scale

____ psychometric scaling

____ psychophysical scaling

____ summated rating scale

    a.   a person scoring higher than another scores as high or higher on each test question

    b.   measurement of theoretical construct with no well defined physical attribute

    c.   measurement of the magnitude of a psychological response to a well defined physical stimulus

    d.   test score is the sum of the weighted responses to each item on the test

5.

____ Guttman scale

____ Likert scale

____ Weber's law

a. cumulative scale
b. $\Delta I/I = K$
c. summated rating scale

6.

____ experimental reliability

____ external validity

____ internal validity

____ parallel form reliability

____ predictive validity

____ reliability

____ split-half reliability

____ statistical reliability

____ test-retest reliability

____ validity

a. all parts of a test measure the same thing
b. alternate forms of a test measure the same attribute
c. consistency of measurement
d. determined by replicating research
e. determined through inferential statistics
f. experimental effects are caused by independent variable, not by confounding
g. experimental effects can be generalized to the population
h. soundness and meaningfulness of measurements
i. stability of test scores over time
j. test scores correlate highly with a criterion measure

7.

____ measurement

____ psychophysics

____ random sampling

____ sample

____ self-report methods

____ theoretical constructs

a. assigning numbers or names to objects or their attributes
b. data that cannot be immediately verified by the researcher
c. every person in a population has the same chance of being included in a research sample
d. intervening variables that link inputs and outputs
e. subset of a population that participates in a research study
f. the study of psychological responses to physical stimuli

PROGRAMMED REVIEW

1. _____ refers to a systematic way of assigning numbers or names to objects and their attributes.

2. The measurement scale that assigns names or numbers solely on the basis of differences among objects is the _____ scale.

3. If a measurement scale can reflect that some objects have more of a certain attribute than other objects, then the measurement scale has the property of _____. The least informative scale with this property is the _____ scale.

4. The Fahrenheit and Centigrade temperature scales are examples of _____ measurement scales because they have _____ _____.

5. Length, height, and weight are measured with _____ scales of measurement, since in addition to having equal units, they also have the property of a _____ _____.

6. Most psychological measurement is at the level of _____ or _____ scales.

7. _____ _____ refers to measuring theoretical constructs when the inputs are well specified (such as loudness), while _____ _____ is used to measure constructs with ill-defined inputs (such as depression.

8. The minimum stimulus intensity required to elicit a detection response is called the _____ _____

9. The smallest amount that the intensity of a stimulus can be noticeably changed is called the _____ _____.

10. Weber found that the size of the difference threshold relative to the intensity of the standard stimulus is _____.

11. In a cumulative, or _____ scale, a person with a higher total score than another person, scores as high or higher that the other person on _____ item of the test.

12. The _____ of _____ is a measure of the adequacy of cumulative scales, and is a ratio of the number of _____ responses to the total number of responses.

13. Likert developed the _____ _____ scale, in which a person's score is the weighted sum of his responses the various items on the test.

14. A good item on a Likert scale shows a _____ _____ with the total test score.

15. _____-_____ methods are those in which data come from personal responses of the respondent, and are usually can not be corroborated by the researcher. This problem threatens the _____ of the measurements.

16. _____ refers to the consistency of measures.

17. The procedure of giving the same test twice in succession over a short time interval is used to determine the _____ - _____ reliability of the test.

18. The form of test reliability determined by administering a single test and looking at the correlations among different sets of items is known as _____ - _____ reliability.

19. _____ statistics are used to determine whether an experimental effect is due to the manipulation of the independent variable, that is, whether the effect is _____ _____.

20. The ability of a statistical test to detect experimental effects, that is, its _____, is increased by _____ the size of the experimental sample.

21. A sampling procedure in which every member of the population has an equal chance of being selected is called a _____ sampling procedure.

22. One way of increasing the representativeness of a sample is to _____ the size of the sample.

EXPERIMENTAL PROJECT

How sensitive are we to differences in thickness of a stack of cards? How does this sensitivity change with the number of cards in the stack?

Prepare three stack of index cards; one of 20, one of 40, and one of 80 cards. These stacks will be your standard stimuli. Prepare three other stacks that are noticeably, but not greatly, thicker than the standard stacks. These thicker stacks will serve are your comparison stimuli.

Present a standard and a comparison stack of cards to a blindfolded participant. At the beginning, the participant should report that the comparison stack feels thicker than the standard. Remove one card at a time from the comparison stack and repeat the feeling of the stack. Repeat this procedure until the participant reports that the stack feel equal, and continue until the comparison stack feels less thick than the standard. Record the number of cards in the comparison stack when the participant changes her response from 'thicker' to 'equal' and also when the response changes from 'equal' to 'thinner'. Repeat this procedure for each of the standard stacks, test each stack about 4 times, and test 3 or 4 participants in this manner.

The difference threshold for thickness is ½ of the difference between the 'thicker-equal' transition, and the 'equal-thinner' transition. Calculate the average difference threshold for each stack size.

According to Weber's law, the difference threshold should be larger for thicker standards. In fact, the ratio of the difference threshold to the size of the standard stack should be constant. Did you find this? How could you compare visual sensitivity to tactile sensitivity for thickness?

EXPERIMENTAL DILEMMA

As discussed in the textbook, in order for a measurement technique to be useful as a scientific tool it is essential that the technique be reliable. A seven category Likert scale for measuring friendliness was devised and administered to a sample of 15-20 people who all rated the same individuals. One week later the same scale was administered to the same sample of people.

It was found that the two sets of scores were not identical. Some people who were rated as very friendly on the first administration were rated as unfriendly a week later. Does this mean that the rating scale is an unreliable measurement technique? Is there a more appropriate way in which to measure the reliability of the rating scale? Is it possible that the rating scale is a reliable tool but the reason for the test-retest results are that peoples' perceptions of the rated individual may have changed over the one week interval?

MULTIPLE CHOICE

1. Which of the following is not one of the types of measurement scales that psychologists are most concerned with?
   a. interval
   b. nominal
   c. ordinal
   d. psychometric
   e. ratio

2. The scale of measurement that has the most stringent requirements is the _____ scale.
   a. interval
   b. nominal
   c. ordinal
   d. ratio

3. The Kelvin scale of temperature is an example of a(n) _____ scale.
    a. interval
    b. nominal
    c. ordinal
    d. ratio

4. The numbers on an athlete's jersey are an example of a(n) _____ scale.
    a. interval
    b. nominal
    c. ordinal
    d. ratio

5. At a horse race the finishing positions are determined by how fast each horse ran the race. Thus, the first finishing horse ran the fastest, the second place horse ran the next fastest, and so on. These finishing positions numbers (i.e., First, Second,...) form a(n) _____ scale.
    a. interval
    b. nominal
    c. ordinal
    d. ratio

6. A theoretical construct is another name for
    a. an independent variable
    b. a dependent variable
    c. a control variable
    d. an intervening variable

7. Psychophysical methods are used to measure theoretical constructs when
    a. the inputs are well defined
    b. the inputs are ill-defined
    c. the outputs are well defined
    d. the outputs are ill-defined

8. Psychometric methods are used to measure theoretical constructs when
    a. the inputs are well defined
    b. the inputs are ill-defined
    c. the outputs are well defined
    d. the outputs are ill-defined

9. Measuring the magnitude of loudness would be done
    a. psychophysically
    b. psychometrically
    c. physiologically
    d. sociometrically

10. Measuring how optimistic someone is would be done
    a. psychophysically
    b. psychometrically
    c. physiologically
    d. sociometrically.

11. The smallest stimulus intensity that can be detected is called the
    a. absolute threshold.
    b. difference threshold.
    c. just-noticeable difference.
    d. minimal stimulus.

12. A threshold based on an observer's ability to detect a single stimulus is called the
    a. difference threshold.
    b. absolute threshold.
    c. mean threshold.
    d. interval uncertainty.

13. According to Weber's law, the size of the difference threshold relative to the standard stimulus is constant for a particular
    a. person.
    b. sensory modality.
    c. stimulus intensity.
    d. all of the above

14. The Guttman and the Likert procedures are both examples of
    a. psychophysical scaling
    b. psychometric scaling
    c. nominal measurement
    d. interval measurement

15. When Terry scores higher than Sandy on a test, then Terry scores higher than or equal to Sandy on every item on the test. This would be true on a
    a. Guttman scale
    b. Likert scale
    c. psychophysical scale
    d. ratio scale

16. Cumulative scales are evaluated with the
    a. coefficient of correlation
    b. coefficient of reproducibility
    c. ordinal function
    d. nominal function

17. In a Likert scale, good test items should
    a. correlate highly with the total test score
    b. measure at the ratio level
    c. show small difference thresholds
    d. have high internal validity

18. If you took a test where you were to show your agreement with a statement by circling one of "SA A U D SD", you would probably be taking a
    a. Guttman scale
    b. Likert scale
    c. Weber scale
    d. Fechner scale

19. A conservative assessment of the level of measurement of Guttman and Likert scales is that they both measure at the _____ level.
    a. nominal
    b. ordinal
    c. interval
    d. ratio

20. When we say that a measure of behavior is reliable, we mean that it is
    a. appropriate.
    b. consistent.
    c. experimental.
    d. useful.

21. A result is said to be statistically reliable if
    a. the result is replicated under conditions that are very different from those of the original experiment.
    b. the number of observations per experimental condition is high.
    c. it is very unlikely that the result occurred by chance.
    d. operational definitions are used to define the dependent variable.

22. The entire set of potential participants is called the _____. The portion of all individuals tested is called a _____ of participants.
    a. population; sample
    b. sample; population
    c. subject pool; random sample
    d. population; population subset

23. Random sampling is done to
    a. increase statistical reliability.
    b. increase sample representativeness.
    c. minimize confounding.
    d. two of the above

24. Random assignment of participants to conditions is done to
    a. increase statistical reliability.
    b. increase sample representativeness.
    c. minimize confounding.
    d. two of the above

25. The greater the number of observations upon which a sample statistic is based,
    a. the greater the reliability of the statistic.
    b. the greater the variability of the statistic.
    c. the greater the error component of the statistic.
    d. none of the above

TRUE-FALSE

1. A ratio scale has a true zero point.

2. A nominal scale uses names instead of numbers.

3. An ordinal scale has only the scale properties of differences and magnitude.

4. An interval scale is the weakest type of measurement scale.

5. If we measure the same thing on several occasions and obtain about the same numbers, we can conclude that our measuring technique is reliable.

6. Split-half reliability involves splitting the sample of subjects into two separate groups and seeing if there is a significant difference between the two groups.

7. Inferential statistics are used to determine the validity of a set of data.

8. Increasing the number of observations we make helps increase the reliability of our results.

9. Random assignment refers to randomly assigning subjects to treatment conditions.

10. Psychophysical methods are techniques used by psychologists to attempt to relate psychological judgment to the characteristics of physical stimuli.

11. Absolute thresholds are based upon relative judgments where a constant comparison stimulus is judged relative to a series of changing stimuli.

12. The Guttman scale is an example of a psychometric method.

13. Advocates of the Guttman scale claim that it measures at the ratio level.

14. Likert scales are often used in psychophysical studies.

15. Inferential statistics play no part in establishing internal validity

16. External reliability arises when the sample mirrors the population of interest.

ESSAY QUESTIONS

1. Averages are easy to calculate, and are often used in situations where they shouldn't be used. Consider your academic grades, and the common overall measure of academic performance, the grade-point average. What assumptions about the quality of measurement are made when a grade-point average is determined? Are these assumptions reasonable? How do you think the valedictorian should be selected?

2. Suppose that you had developed a Likert scale to measure generosity. What would be necessary to demonstrate that your scale was reliable? valid?

ANSWERS

KEY TERM MATCHING

1. a, b, c
2. c, d, b, a
3. b, c, a, d
4. a, b, c, d
5. a, c, b
6. d, g, f, b, j, c, a, e, i, h
7. a, f, c, e, b, d

PROGRAMMED REVIEW
1. measurement; (p. 188)
2. nominal; (p. 189)
3. magnitude, ordinal; (p. 190)
4. interval; (p. 190)
5. ratio; (p. 190)

6. ordinal, interval; (p. 191)
7. psychophysical scaling, psychometric scaling ; (p. 193)
8. absolute threshold; (p. 194)
9. difference threshold; (p. 194)
10. constant; (p. 194)
11. Guttman; (p. 195)
12. coefficient of reproducibility, appropriate; (p. 196)
13. summated rating; (p. 198)
14. positive correlation; (p. 199)
15. self-report, validity; (p. 200)
16. reliability; (p. 201)
17. test-retest; (p. 203)
18. split-half; (p. 203)
19. inferential, statistically reliable ; (p. 204)
20. power, increasing; (p. 206)
21. random; (p. 206)
22. increase; (p. 206)

MULTIPLE CHOICE

1. d; (p. 189)

2. d; (p. 190)

3. a; (p. 190)

4. b; (p. 189)

5. c; (p. 190)

6. d; (p. 192)

7. a; (p. 193)

8. b; (p. 193)

9. a; (p. 193)

10. b; (p. 193)

11. a; (p. 194)

12. b; (p. 194)

13. b; (p. 194)

14. b; (p. 195)

15. a; (p. 195)

16. b; (p. 196)

17. a; (p. 199)

18. b; (p. 198)

19. b; (p. 200)

20. b; (p. 201)

21. c; (p. 204)

22. a; (p. 205)

23. b; (p. 206)

24. c; (p. 207)

25. a; (p. 206)

TRUE-FALSE

1. T; (p. 190)	2. F; (p. 189)	3. T; (p. 190)
4. F; (p. 190)	5. T; (p. 201)	6. F; (p. 203)
7. F; (p. 204)	8. T; (p. 206)	9. T; (p. 206)
10. T; (p. 193)	11. F; (p. 194)	12. T; (p. 195)
13. T; (p. 197)	14. F; (p. 198)	15. T; (p. 207)
16. T; (p. 206)		

CHAPTER 9.

Experimental Design

SUMMARY

I.   Internal Validity in Experiments
  A.   In a properly designed experiment, behavioral effects result solely from
        manipulations of the independent variables. This means that experimental
        results are **internally valid**.
II.   Experimental Design
  A.   **Between-Subjects Designs**
    1.   Each individual participant is assigned to one of the treatment
          conditions.
    2.   There is no chance of one treatment condition contaminating
          another since each participant serves in only one condition.
    3.   If the participants assigned to the different groups are not
          equivalent, participant differences are confounded with levels of the
          independent variable.
    4.   Procedures to equate the groups include
      a.   **Matching**
        (1)   procedure
          (a)   Sets of equivalent subject are identified, often
                 using a pretest.
          (b)   One member of each set is randomly assigned to
                 each treatment condition.
        (2)   problems
          (a)   experimenter can't match on all relevant variables,
                 and may not know what to match on.

        (b)   **subject attrition**, the loss of one or more participants from the study, will result in unequal groups.

  b. **Randomization**

     (1) Subjects are assigned randomly to the various treatment conditions.

     (2) This procedure is the preferred method of equating groups of participants, since each participant has an equal and unbiased chance of being in any treatment condition.

B. **Within-Subjects Designs**

  1. Each participant is tested in every experimental condition.

  2. Advantages of within-subjects designs include

    a. efficiency of research

    b. the treatment groups are guaranteed to be equivalent

  3. **Carryover effects** are a threat to the internal validity of experiments that use within-subjects designs.

    a. Carryover effects occur when the effects of being tested in one condition carry over and influence the behavior measured in another condition.

    b. carryover effects can be minimized by

      (1) randomly determining the sequence of treatments received by different participants.

      (2) using **counterbalancing** procedures to determine the order of treatments received by every participant.

        (a) Complete counterbalancing requires that all possible orders of treatments be used for the same number of participants. This is impractical with a large number of treatments.

        (b) Incomplete counterbalancing presents each treatment equally often at each stage of the experiment. A **Latin-square design** is a convenient way to generate the required treatment orders.

        (c) A **balanced Latin square** is a special kind of Latin square in which each treatment precedes and follows every other treatment equally often.

C.   **Mixed Designs** are often appropriate for experiments with more than one independent variable. In these designs some independent variables are tested between subjects, and the others are tested within subjects.

III. **Control Conditions** in an experiment provide a **baseline** against which the level in interest of the independent variable can be compared.

IV. Choosing an Experimental Design

    A.   Carryover Effects

        1.   If a experimental treatment is likely to produce a permanent on long-lasting effect on participants, a between-subjects design should be used.

        2.   A within-subjects design should be used to study changes in behavior over time.

    B.   **Individual Differences**

        1.   refers to the various ways in which people are different from each other.

        2.   if large individual differences are likely to influence the dependent variable, a within-subjects design might be preferable to a between-subjects design..

KEY TERM MATCHING

1.

___ balanced Latin square

___ between-subjects design

___ Latin-square design

___ within-subjects design

a.   each participant receives every treatment

b.   each participant receives only one treatment

c.   each treatment precedes and follows every other treatment equally often

d.   every treatment appears equally often at each stage in the experiment

2.

___ counterbalancing

___ matching

___ randomization

a.   less preferred way of establishing equivalent groups

b.   preferred way of establishing equivalent groups

c.   used to minimize carryover effects

3.

___ control condition

___ individual differences

___ internal validity

___ subject attrition

a. provides a baseline for comparison with the treatment of interest

b. why treatment groups may not be equivalent

c. in principle, a property of the experimental method

d. a problem, especially when matching is used to form equivalent groups

PROGRAMMED REVIEW

1. A good experiment allows the researcher to state that changes in the independent variable _____ the observed changes in the dependent variable.

2. Experiments that lead to valid results are said to be _____ valid.

3. In the "executive monkey" experiments reported by Brady and his colleagues, the independent variable was (describe briefly)

   _____

   _____

4. Weiss (1971) showed that animals which respond at a _____ rate are likely to get ulcers, whether they are helpless or in control.

5. An experimental design in which each participant receives all levels of the independent variable is called a _____-subjects design.

6. The first design decision an experimenter must make is how to assign _____ to the various levels of the independent variable.

7. An experiment in which each participant is assigned to a particular level of the independent variable is called a _____-subjects design.

8. In any between-subjects experiment the researcher must strive to minimize differences among the _____ _____ that may exist before the experiment begins.

9. When the technique of matching is used to equate the various treatment groups the experimenter is trying to match on the basis of important _____ characteristics.

10. Matching is done on the basis of the most likely _____ variables.

11. When one or more of the participant s in an experiment do not complete the experiment this introduces the problem of subject _____.

12. The technique known as _____ is used to ensure the formation of equivalent groups of participants by giving each participant an equal opportunity to serve in any condition of the experiment.

13. Experimental design is concerned with the logic of _____ experiments.

14. The preferred technique for assigning participants to experimental conditions is the _____ technique.

15. The _____-subjects design is generally the more efficient design.

16. If participation in one treatment condition is likely to affect performance in another treatment condition, then we would say that _____ effects pose a problem in this experiment.

17. The problem with using randomization to minimize carry-over effects is that a large number of _____ are required.

18. Complete _____ ensures that all possible treatment orders are used.

19. In a balanced _____-_____ design every experimental condition is preceded and followed equally often by every other condition.

20. If two Latin squares were needed to counterbalance the order of treatment presentations, than there must have been a(n) _____ number of treatment conditions.

21. A _____ design is one that employs both within- and between-subjects variable.

22. In its simplest form, a _____ group is the group that does not receive the levels of interest of the independent variable.

23. A control condition provides a _____ against which some other variable of the experiment may be compared.

24. Suppose your independent variable is likely to exert a permanent effect on your participant s. What type of design should you employ in this case?

    _____

25. What type of design should be employed if there are large individual differences among the participants in your sample?

    _____

EXPERIMENTAL PROJECT

If a person is asked to solve several problems in succession, all of which are solvable by one procedure, the person will tend to continue using this procedure, even when a much simpler solution to the problem exists. Luchins (1942) performed a number of experiments in which he demonstrated this effect of Einstellung (mental set). In this experimental project you are going to replicate part of Luchins' original demonstration, after which you will be given a chance to see if you can design a better research project for examining the effect of mental set on problem solving.

You will need at least two volunteers for this experiment, although six or eight would probably be a more appropriate sample size. Divide your participants into two groups of equal size. (Question: How are you going to assign participants to groups? Maybe you had better read the whole Experimental Project and then decided how to assign participants!) The participants will be told that their task is to obtain a specific volume of water, using empty jars with varying capacities as their measuring devices. There will be 8 problems in all, and these are listed below.

Problem: Given these jars, obtain the following amounts:

| Problem | Given Jars of these Capacities | | | Obtain |
	A	B	C	
1.00	29.00	3.00	--	20.00
2.00	21.00	127.00	3.00	100.00
3.00	14.00	163.00	25.00	99.00
4.00	18.00	43.00	10.00	5.00
5.00	9.00	42.00	6.00	21.00
6.00	20.00	59.00	4.00	31.00
7.00	23.00	49.00	3.00	20.00
8.00	15.00	39.00	3.00	18.00

(These numbers represent the quart-capacity of the jars.)

All participants are given the following information. The participants' task is to use the 3 jars available for that problem to obtain exactly the amount of water needed to solve the problem. There is an unlimited water supply.

Participants in both the experimental group and control groups are first shown how to solve problem number 1: Fill the 29 quart jar, then use that jar to fill (and then empty) the 3 quart jar 3 times, thus leaving exactly 20 quarts of water in the larger jar.

Participants in the experimental group then receive problems 2 through 8. The experimenter will demonstrate how to solve problem 2 (i.e., fill jar b, use this jar to fill jar once and jar c twice, thus leaving 100 quarts of water in jar b; 127 - 21 - 3 - 3 = 100). The experimental participants are then allowed to solve problems 3 through 8.

The control group participants move directly from problem 1 to problems 7 and 8.

Ask your participants to describe the method they used to solve problems 7 and 8. On the basis of these descriptions you may classify how your participants solved the problems, by the indirect route (i.e., 49 - 23 - 3 - 3 Problem 7) or the direct route (i.e., 23 - 3 Problem 7).

The dependent variable in this experiment might be the percentage of participants who use a direct route for both problems 7 and 8. Which of your two groups showed a higher percentage of direct solutions? Do you think that the control group in this experiment was the appropriate one? Can you think of another possible control condition? (Hint: How many problems in all were given to each group.) Could the effect of mental set be studied using a within-subjects design? Can you think of another dependent variable that might be used in this experiment?

REFERENCE

Luchins, A.S. (1942). Mechanization in problem solving. Psychological Monographs. 54, No. 6 (Whole No. 248).

EXPERIMENTAL DILEMMA

A researcher is interested in studying the effect of environmental stress on the performance of various mental tasks. The environmental stressor is the temperature level in the experimental chamber. The researcher selects three different temperatures (40 F, 70 F, and 90 F) for the levels of stress to be included in the experiment. Since this is an experiment involving some risk to the participants, the researcher employs male undergraduates to serve as participants. The mental task selected for the first experiment is a choice reaction time task in which one of four stimulus lights comes on and the participant is to respond by pressing one of four buttons as quickly as possible. The researcher thinks that stressful environments will make participants respond faster.

The researcher tests each participant in each condition during the 90 minute testing session. Each participant is first tested in the 70 condition, then the 90 condition, and finally in the 40 condition. Participants receive 30 trials in each condition.

The results showed that the participants mean reaction times for the three conditions were as follows:

Temperature	Mean Reaction Time
40 F	430 msec
70 F	525 msec
90 F	487 msec

Statistical analysis of the mean reaction times revealed that each of the three conditions was reliably different from the other two conditions. The researcher concluded that thermal stress improves reaction time. Do you agree with this conclusion?

MULTIPLE CHOICE

1. In principle, experiments are designed to allow statements about
   a. causation.
   b. contiguity.
   c. correlation.
   d. relatedness.
   e. both c and d

2. The results of the early "executive-monkey" studies were invalid because
   a. the shocks used to induce stress were themselves capable of producing ulcers.
   b. the subjects assigned to the "executive" and "co-worker" conditions were different even prior to the beginning of the experiment.
   c. it is not valid to compare directly the results of animal research and human behavior.
   d. the differences between the experimental and control groups reflect correlations and not true causal relations.

3. In a simple between-subjects experimental design, each participant is given _____ level of the independent variable; in a within-subjects design each participant is given _____ level of the independent variable.
   a. one; one
   b. each; one
   c. one; each
   d. each; each

4. The purpose of good experimental design is to
   a. minimize extraneous or uncontrolled variation.
   b. come up with interesting research ideas.
   c. increase the likelihood that an experiment will produce internally valid results.
   d. avoid carry-over effects.
   e. both a and c

5. Which of the following is not a problem associated with between-subjects designs?
   a. the between-subjects design is a conservative design
   b. carry-over effect
   c. unequal treatment groups prior to the introduction of the independent variable
   d. subject attrition

6. The difference between a within-subjects design and a between-subjects design is that
   a. fewer participans are needed in a between-subjects design.
   b. each participant serves as his or her own control in within-subject designs.
   c. confounding cannot occur with between-subjects designs.
   d. a given participant's behavior is measured only once in within-subjects designs.

7. A major disadvantage of between-subjects designs is that
   a. the effect of one treatment may alter the effectiveness of later treatments.
   b. participant differences may obscure treatment effects.
   c. one must use fewer independent variable.
   d. one can use only one dependent variable.

8. In order to obtain equivalent groups in between-subjects designs, you can
   a. randomly assign participants to the various treatment groups.
   b. use each participant as his or her own control.
   c. attempt to match participants on variables that are relevant.
   d. all of the above
   e. both a and c

9. One reason for preferring randomization to matching for establishing group equivalence is that
   a. we do not know all the relevant variables to match.
   b. randomization involves less confounding.
   c. counterbalancing does not require randomization.
   d. randomization guarantees group equivalence.

10. For between-subjects designs, randomization and matching are techniques used in an attempt to
    a. prevent treatment carry-over effects.
    b. ensure that the groups are equivalent at the start of the experiment.
    c. minimize experimenter effects.
    d. minimize demand characteristics.
    e. both c and d

11. In within-subjects designs, counterbalancing is used to
    a. enable the experimenter to evaluate possible treatment order effects.
    b. assign participants to treatment groups.
    c. eliminate the effects of treatment order.
    d. all of the above

12. In a completely counterbalanced experimental design
    a. each group of participants receives a different treatment.
    b. every participant receives every treatment.
    c. all possible treatment orders are used.
    d. the treatment orders are randomized.
    e. both b and c

13. In a balanced Latin square design
    a. each treatment appears once in each row.
    b. each treatment appears once in each column.
    c. each treatment precedes and follows every other treatment equally often.
    d. all of the above
    e. both a and b

14. A mixed design is one in which
    a. there is one independent and one dependent variable.
    b. at least one independent variable is tested within-subjects and the other independent variable(s) is (are) tested between-subjects.
    c. one independent variable is manipulated and the other independent variable(s) is (are) controlled.
    d. each participant receives a mixture of treatment conditions.

15. A control group or a control condition is included in an experiment to
    a. evaluate experimenter effects and demand effects.
    b. provide a baseline against which the variable of interest can be compared.
    c. prevent ceiling or floor effects.
    d. increase the generalizability of the results.

16. In an experiment designed to investigate the effects of alcohol on appetite, if drinks X and Y contain 0.5 and 1.0 ounces of vodka in orange juice, respectively, and drink Z contains only orange juice then the control group in the experiment should receive
    a. drink X.
    b. drink Y.
    c. drink Z.
    d. nothing to drink.
    e. X, Y, and Z in a counterbalanced order.

TRUE-FALSE

____ 1. Experiments are internally valid in principle.

____ 2. A major concern in experimental design is preventing carryover effects in within-subjects designs.

____ 3. The first design decision an experimenter must make is what levels of the independent variable should be used.

____ 4. A within-subjects design is more conservative than a between-subjects design.

____ 5. If an experimenter suspects that the effects of one treatment may linger on to alter behavior in a later condition, then she should use a counterbalanced within-subjects design.

____ 6. The technique of counterbalancing is used in within-subjects designs to reduce the effects of treatment order.

____ 7. One difficulty with matching is that the experimenter cannot know all the potentially relevant dimensions on which to match subjects.

____ 8. Subject attrition has a less detrimental effect when group characteristics are determined by an unbiased procedure, as compared to a matching procedure.

____ 9. Random assignment of subjects to conditions guarantees that treatment groups will be equal prior to the administration of the independent variable.

____ 10. Within-subjects designs are generally more efficient than between-subjects designs.

____ 11. Carry-over effects are eliminated in a completely counterbalanced design.

____ 12. Unless the number of experimental conditions is greater than 7, a single balanced Latin square is sufficient for counterbalancing treatment orders within an experiment.

____ 13. Counterbalancing can be used for assigning treatment orders as well as determining the order of testing when more than one independent variable is used.

____ 14. The control group is the group that does not receive the levels of interest of the independent variable.

ESSAY QUESTIONS

1. Briefly describe the design flaw in the original "executive monkey" studies. How could these experiments have been redesigned in order to avoid the design flaw?

2. Discuss the advantages and disadvantages of between-subjects and within-subjects designs.

3.   Describe what is meant by subject attrition. How can subject attrition affect the results of an experiment? What types of experimental designs would you expect to be least affected by subject attrition?

ANSWERS

KEY TERM MATCHING

1. c, b, d, a   2. c, a, b   3. a, b, c, d

PROGRAMMED REVIEW

1.   cause; (p. 214)
2.   internally; (p. 214)
3.   ability to postpone shock; (p. 214)
4.   high; (p. 215)
5.   within; (p. 217)
6.   participants; (p. 217)
7.   between; (p. 217)
8.   treatment groups; (p. 218)
9.   participant; (p. 218)
10.   confounding; (p. 218)
11.   attrition; (p. 219)
12.   randomization; (p. 219)
13.   arranging; (p. 219)
14.   randomization; (p. 219)
15.   within; (p. 220)
16.   carryover; (p. 220)
17.   participants; (p. 221)
18.   counterbalancing; (p. 221)
19.   Latin square; (p. 223)
20.   odd; (p. 224)
21.   mixed; (p. 227)
22.   control; (p. 225)
23.   baseline; (p. 226)
24.   between-subjects; (p. 227)
25.   within-subjects; (p. 228)

MULTIPLE CHOICE

1. a (p. 214)   2. b (p. 215)   3. c (p. 217)

4. e (p. 216)   5. b (p. 220)   6. b (p. 218)

7. b (p. 218)   8. e (p. 218)   9. a (p. 218)

10. b (p. 218)   11. a (p. 221)   12. e (p. 221)

13. d (p. 223)   14. b (p. 227)   15. b (p. 225)

16. d (p. 225)

TRUE-FALSE

1. F (p. 214)   2. T (p. 220)   3. F (p. 217)

4. F (p. 218)   5. F (p. 227)   6. T (p. 221)

7. T (p. 218)   8. T (p. 219)   9. F (p. 219)

10. T (p. 220)   11. F (p. 221)   12. F (p. 223)

13. T (p. 221)   14. T (p. 225)

CHAPTER 10.

Complex Experimentation

SUMMARY

I.   Complex experiments provide
     A.   increased control,
     B.   greater efficiency,
     C.   greater ecological validity, since real world behavior is generally influenced
          by many factors.
II. Factorial Designs
     A.   examine all possible combinations of levels of all independent variables.
     B.   A study of the sleeper effect was used to illustrate a factorial design
          1.   The **sleeper effect** refers to the increased efficacy of a persuasive
               message with the passage of time.
          2.   In order to obtain the sleeper effect, **a discounting cue** must be
               presented with the original message. The discounting cue causes one to
               distrust the persuasive message.
          3.   A 2 x 2 factorial design was used to investigate whether presenting the
               discounting cue before or after the persuasive message would influence
               the magnitude of the sleeper effect.
               a.   One of the independent variables was the *placement* of the
                    discounting cue; the levels were *before* and *after*.
               b.   The other independent variable was the *delay* between the
                    message and an opinion rating about the topic of the message; the
                    levels were *0 delay* and *6-weeks delay*.
               c.   Four groups of subjects were tested, one in each combination of
                    these levels; before-0, before-6-weeks, after-0, and after-6-weeks.

    d.   The **main effect** of placement was found to be small; overall there was a trivial difference between ratings obtained with the before and after discounting cue.

    e.   The main effect of delay was appreciable; ratings were higher with the 6-week delay than with the 0 delay. This is the sleeper effect.

    f.   An **interaction** was found; a much greater sleeper effect was found when the discounting cue was placed after the persuasive message. An interaction occurs when the effects of one independent variable are not the same at different levels of another independent variable.

C. Patterns of Interaction

    1.   In a factorial experiment, main effects and interactions are entirely independent of each other; any combination of main effects and interactions might occur, and the nature of the interaction is not predictable from knowledge of the main effects.

    2.   A crossover interaction is an important type of interaction.

       a.   The lines on a graph cross over each other.

       b.   This kind of interaction cannot be explained by errors in measurement or scaling of the dependent variable.

D. Control in Between-Subjects Factorial Designs

    1.   The major concern is that *equivalent* groups of subjects are assigned to the various treatment combinations.

    2.   Random selection, random assignment, Latin squares, and matching are techniques that are used to try to create equivalent groups.

       a.   a **random-groups design** refers to the unbiased assignment of subjects to groups.

       b.   a matched-groups design in one in which matched sets of subjects are formed, and a member from each set is randomly assigned to each treatment combination.

III. Complex Within-Subjects Designs

A. Within-Subject designs provide

    1.   greater economy than between-subject designs, and

    2.   guarantee group equivalence.

B. A within-subjects factorial design is often called a **treatments x treatments x subjects design**; each subject is tested in all treatment combinations.

C. Control in Complex Within-Subjects Designs

    1.   The major concern is that carryover effects do not contaminate the results.

2. **Block randomization** is used to control carryover effects by presenting each of the treatment combinations in a random order, and repeating this procedure for as many blocks as desired.

3. Other means of dealing with carryover effects include complete randomization and counterbalancing.

IV. **Mixed Designs** have one or more between-subjects independent variables, and one or more within-subjects independent variables.

KEY TERM MATCHING

1.

____ 2 x 2 factorial design

____ block randomization

____ matched-group designs

____ mixed designs

____ random-groups design

____ treatment x treatment x subject design

a. all conditions are presented in a random order before any condition is repeated.

b. between-subjects factorial design with 2 independent variables, each with two levels

c. has at least one between-subjects and at least one within-subjects independent variable

d. sets of similar participants are randomly divided among the treatments

e. participants are assigned randomly to groups

f. within-subjects factorial design

2.

____ crossover interaction

____ discounting cue

____ interaction

____ main effects

____ sleeper effect

a. overall differences in the dependent variable among the levels of an independent variable

b. particularly convincing form of an interaction

c. the effect of one independent variable is not the same at each level of a second independent variable

d. information that encourages disbelief of another message

e. the increase of effectiveness of a persuasive message with the passage of time.

PROGRAMMED REVIEW

___ 1. Multifactor experiments are likely to have better _____ validity than single-factor experiments.

___ 2. Complex multifactor experiments allow the researcher to make complex causal statements which should increase _____ validity.

___ 3. The phenomenon of an increase in the effectiveness of a persuasive message is called the _____ effect.

___ 4. To obtain a sleeper effect, the persuasive message must be accompanied by a _____ _____.

___ 5. In a 2 x 2 factorial design there are two _____ variables, each with two _____.

___ 6. A factorial experiment includes all possible combinations of all levels of the _____ _____.

___ 7. The effect of a single independent variable is called a _____ effect.

___ 8. An _____ effect occurs when the effects of one independent variable depend upon the level of another independent variable.

___ 9. In an ideal experiment, participants would be randomly _____ and then randomly _____ to treatment conditions.

___ 10. In a between-subjects design we want to make sure that the characteristics of the _____ are not confounded with group membership.

___ 11. Two techniques for achieving unbiased assignment of participants to conditions are to _____ assign participants to treatment conditions or to use a balanced _____ _____ to determine group membership.

___ 12. In general researchers try to avoid experimental designs in which potential _____ variables can interact with the independent variable(s).

___ 13. A design in which the assignment of participants to conditions is unbiased is called a _____ - _____ design.

___ 14. In a matched-groups design the _____ are matched on a potentially important variable.

____ 15. A _____-subjects design automatically controls for individual differences.

____ 16. A _____-subjects design requires fewer subjects than does a comparable _____-subjects design.

____ 17. The reduced number of participants tested in a within-subjects design may require that the experimenter increase the number of observations per _____.

____ 18. When there are two independent variables there are _____ possible main effect(s) and _____ possible interaction(s).

____ 19. Whenever an independent variable is manipulated within-subjects there is a possibility of potential _____ effects.

____ 20. Carryover effects can be guarded against by _____ or a _____ randomization in which the order of treatments would be randomized two or more times.

____ 21. In a _____ randomized design every condition is tested before a particular condition is tested again.

____ 22. _____ designs have one or more between-subjects independent variables and one or more within-subjects variable.

EXPERIMENTAL PROJECT

Some memory researchers have found that information is better remembered when the presentations of study material are spaced apart from one another than when the presentations are massed together. That is, you will probably do better on an exam if you study the test material periodically throughout the course than if you just cram the night before the test. As an illustration of this general principle, conduct a study in which you manipulate spaced versus massed presentation as one of your independent variables. In order to better understand the concept of multifactor designs, add another manipulation of type of study material, namely whether study words occur with high or low frequency in natural language. (Lists of high and low frequency words may be obtained from the Kucera and Francis word norms found in Computational analysis of present-day American English. Providence, RI: Brown University Press, 1967.) Manipulate spaced versus massed presentation between subjects and test word frequency as a within-subjects factor.

The study material for all subjects will consist of a 100 word list - half of the words should be high frequency items and half should be low frequency items. Test the same number of people in the spaced and massed groups and equate total study time across the two groups. participants in the spaced group should be given the time lapse between presentations, which should be the same for all participants in the group. Give a 10 minute free recall test immediately following the third presentation. Give the massed group the stimulus list and have them study it for 30 minutes. Following study test them in exactly the same manner as the spaced group.

Score the data for a general measure of number of words recalled for the spaced versus massed conditions and for number of high frequency words versus number of low frequency words recalled across groups. These measure will allow you to assess main effects. You will also need a breakdown of the number of high and low frequency words recalled in each study group in order to look at interaction effects. Plot the number of words recalled as a function of word frequency and study condition. Do you find any main effects? Is there any evidence of an interaction? Did it appear that ceiling effects or floor effects might be present in your experiment? What do these results suggest to you concerning your present study strategies?

EXPERIMENTAL DILEMMAS

1.   An experimenter examined the effects of test expectancy (i.e., expecting a recall test of a recognition test) on performance of different types of tests as a function of the type of material to be learned. The study words were varied as to their imageability. That is, high imagery words were those for which participantss could readily form a mental image (e.g., apple) and low imagery words were items for which mental images could not be easily formed (e.g., decision). All of those variables were manipulated between-subjects. Thus the design was a 2 (test expectancy: recall versus recognition) x 2 (test type: recall versus recognition) x 2 (imagery: high versus low) multifactor design. Participants were given a 25 item word list to study overnight and were told that they would be given either a recall or recognition test the next day. Half of the participants were told to expect a recall test and half were told to expect recognition. In addition, half of the participants were given a list of low imagery words and half studied high imagery words. Participants were tested upon returning to the laboratory. Half of the participants received the type of test that they expected and half were given the unexpected test type. The following results were obtained. The numbers represent percent correct on the memory tests.

	LOW IMAGERY TEST GIVEN		HIGH IMAGERY TEST GIVEN	
TEST EXPECTED	RECALL	RECOGNITION	RECALL	RECOGNITION
RECALL	70.00	75.00	99.00	99.00
RECOGNITION	40.00	85.00	92.00	98.00

There were main effects of test type, test expectancy, and imagery. There was a test type x test expectancy interaction and there was a three way interaction of test type, test expectancy, and imagery. The experimenter concluded that performance on recognition tests was superior to performance on recall tests and that participants performed better in general when led to expect recall than when expecting recognition. She also argued that high imagery words were better remembered than low imagery words. Furthermore, performance was enhanced when the type of test given matched the type of test expected. With regard to the three way interaction, the experimenter concluded that when participants study low imagery words recognition performance is superior to recall when participants expect recall but that there is no such difference when high imagery words are studied.

Is there anything wrong with the design or procedures used in this experiment? Do you agree with the conclusion? How would you design an experiment to test the hypotheses under consideration?

2. A researcher hypothesizes that people will be able to recall words better when given instructions to form images of the words during presentation than if given no special instructions. In addition the experimenter wishes to examine the effects of delaying the recall test for different periods of time. It is expected that recall performance will drop with increased delay but it is not known how this variable might interact with the encoding manipulation. Two groups of participants are tested: The imagery group is instructed to form mental images of each word as it is presented, but the No Imagery group is given no explicit instructions. All participants are presented with the same list of 50 concrete nouns at the rate of 10 seconds each. Each of the two groups is divided so that half of the participants are given a free recall test one week later. All participants are allowed 5 minutes for the

recall test. The results obtained are presented below.

	INSTRUCTIONS	
DELAY	IMAGERY	NO IMAGERY
1 HOUR	75%	50%
1 WEEK	50%	25%

There was a main effect of instruction condition and of delay condition but there was no instruction x delay interaction. From these data the experimenter concluded that memory performance is enhanced when subjects are instructed to form mental images of input items and that performance decreases as the delay between input and test increases, but that the delay manipulation does not differentially affect performance as a function of input condition. Do you agree with these conclusions? If not, why?

MULTIPLE CHOICE

1. Which of the following is not a reason for doing multifactor experiments instead of several single-factor experiments?
   a. increase the internal validity of the experiments
   b. increase the generality of the results
   c. fewer observations per participant are required in a multifactor experiment
   d. multifactor experiments attempt to match the complexity of forces that combine to influence our thought and behavior
   e. all of the above

2. A factorial experiment
   a. is a between-subjects design.
   b. involves testing all possible combinations of all levels of each independent variable.
   c. allows the researcher to observe interaction effects.
   d. all of the above
   e. both b and c

3. In a 3 x 3 factorial experiment, how many effects can we determine?
    a. 2
    b. 3
    c. 4
    d. 6
    e. 9

4. In a 3 x 2 between-subjects design, there are _____ independent groups and each subject serves in _____ conditions in the experiment.
    a. 5; 1
    b. 5; 2
    c. 6; 1
    d. 6; 2
    e. 6; 6

5. According to the dissociation hypothesis explanation of the sleeper effect,
    a. there is less opinion change over time.
    b. the link between the message and discounting cue strengthens over time.
    c. the message is remembered while the discounting cue is forgotten.
    d. the discounting cue is easier to retrieve.

6. What does it mean when we say that a main effect was obtained in a between-subjects factorial experiment?
    a. The scores obtained under one level of an independent variable were different than the scores obtained under another level of that independent variable.
    b. The mean score from one level of an independent variable was different from the mean score of one level of a different independent variable.
    c. Overall, one independent variable had a larger effect on the dependent variable than did the other independent variables.
    d. The effect of the independent variable was different for different dependent variables.

7. Which of the following describes an interaction effect?
    a. The scores obtained at one level of the independent variable were different than the scores obtained at another level of the independent variable.
    b. The observed effect of one independent variable depends on the level of other independent variables.
    c. The effect of one independent variable was larger for one dependent variable than for another.
    d. The nature of an interaction can only be described when the type of experimental design is known.

8. In a factorial experiment, the number of factors is the number of _____ variables and the number of levels is the number of instances of each _____ variable tested in the experiment.
    a. dependent; dependent
    b. independent; independent
    c. dependent; independent
    d. independent; dependent

9. An interaction effect occurs when
    a. performance in one condition is superior to that in another condition.
    b. performance changes across levels of the independent variable.
    c. the effect of the dependent variable reflects performance in more than one experimental condition.
    d. the effects of one independent variable change depending on the level of another independent variable

10. An experiment with two factors and two levels of each factor with all possible combinations of these factors is called a _____ factorial.
    a. 2 x 2
    b. 2 x 2 x 2
    c. 2
    d. 2 x 4 x 8

11. Complex multifactor experiments
    a. can be efficient.
    b. can produce results that are difficult to interpret.
    c. allow us to observe both main effects and interaction effects.
    d. all of the above

12. An experiment in which the effects of more than one independent variable are examined simultaneously is called a _____ experiment.
    a. mixed factor
    b. multifactor
    c. single factor
    d. within-subjects

13. When experimental results are presented in a figure, the presence of an interaction is indicated by:
    a. positive or negative slope of the lines.
    b. one line that is higher than another.
    c. two (or more) lines that are not parallel to the x-axis.
    d. two (or more) lines that are not parallel to the y-axis.
    e. lines that are not parallel with one another.

14. In a between-subjects factorial design the researcher must make an effort to:
    a. ensure that the characteristics of the participant are not confounded with group membership.
    b. equate treatment conditions across the independent groups.
    c. administer all levels of the independent variable to each participant.
    d. control for carry-over effects.

15. The within-subjects design is often used instead of a between-subjects design because
    a. of carry-over effects.
    b. the within-subjects design requires fewer subjects.
    c. the within-subjects design controls for individual differences.
    d. there is not a problem in determining which participants receive the identical treatment orders.
    e. both b and c

16. Compared to a between-subjects random group factorial design, a within-subjects factorial design
    a. requires matching participants on relevant variables.
    b. requires fewer participants.
    c. requires more observations per participant.
    d. all of the above
    e. both b and c

17. Under which of the following conditions would you want to avoid using a treatment x treatment x subjects design?
    a. there are large differences between individual participants.
    b. there are only a small number of participants available for participation in the experiment
    c. participation in one treatment condition may affect performance levels in another condition
    d. many observations can be obtained from a single participant
    e. all of the above

18. A mixed-design experiment is one that contains
    a. an independent variable and a subject variable.
    b. repeated measures and within-subjects factors.
    c. two independent variables that produced an interaction.
    d. at least one between-subject, and at least one within-subject independent variable.

19. The results of the Dewing and Hetherington (1974) study suggest that
    a. imagery value of the solution word affects anagram solution time.
    b. the type of hint given may influence anagram solution time.
    c. for high imagery words a semantic clue aids anagram solution more than a structural clue.
    d. for low imagery words a structural clue aids anagram solution more than a semantic clue.
    e. all of the above

20. If a 6 x 6 balanced Latin square were used to determine the order of presentation of 6 treatment conditions, in what multiples would the experimenter have to test subjects in?
    a. 6
    b. 12
    c. 18
    d. 36
    e. 216

TRUE-FALSE

____ 1. Multifactor experiments are more likely to have ecological validity than single-factor experiments.

____ 2. If possible researchers should start off research in a new area by employing multifactor experiments since these designs are more efficient than single-factor experiments.

____ 3. In a within-subjects design the number of groups of subjects is equal to the product of number of levels of the independent variable times the number of independent variables.

____ 4. In a main effect one dependent variable shows a different pattern of results than the other dependent variable.

____ 5. In order to obtain an interaction at least one of the factors involved in the interaction must have produced a significant main effect.

____ 6. Main effects are more revealing than interaction effects.

____ 7. In a random groups design the experimenter attempts to reduce random variability by equating subjects on variable other than the independent variable(s).

____ 8. Within-subjects designs typically require few observations per subject because each subject serves as their own control.

____ 9. The primary dangers inherent in treatment x treatment x subjects design are carryover effects.

____ 10. Across test trials, block randomization would be less likely than complete randomization to confound test order and condition.

____ 11. In a within-subjects design, the advantage of using a balanced Latin square to assign treatment orders (as opposed to randomization procedures) is that with the Latin square method each treatment would precede and follow every other treatment equally often.

ESSAY QUESTIONS

1. Briefly discuss the advantages and disadvantages of using multifactor experimental designs.

2. Describe several conditions under which it would be preferable to use a between-subjects design. When would a within-subjects design be preferable?

3. Consider an experimental design similar to the one in the chapter in which the discounting cue and delay of rating are manipulated in a factorial design. Make up patterns of results (different from those reported in the text) to sketch the following:

    a. Main effects of both variables with no interaction.

    b. An interaction effect but no main effects.

    c. Only one main effect and a significant interaction.

ANSWERS

KEY TERM MATCHING

1. b, a, d, c, e, f   2. b, c, d, a, e

PROGRAMMED REVIEW

1. external; (p. 236)
2. external; (p. 236)
3. sleeper; (p. 236)
4. discounting cue; (p. 236)
5. independent, levels; (p. 237)
6. independent variables; (p. 237)
7. main; (p. 238)
8. interaction; (p. 240)
9. selected, assigned; (p. 244)
10. participants; (p. 244)
11. randomly, Latin square; (p. 245)
12. confounding; (p. 245)
13. random-groups; (p. 245)
14. participants; (p. 245)
15. within; (p. 246)
16. within-between; (p. 246)
17. participant; (p. 246)
18. two, one; (p. 242)
19. carryover; (p. 249)
20. counterbalancing, block; (p. 249)
21. block; (p. 249)
22. mixed; (p. 236)

MULTIPLE CHOICE

1. a;(p. 236)	2. e;(p. 237)	3. b ;(p.238)
4. c;(p. 237)	5. c;(p. 237)	6. a;(p. 238)
7. b;(p. 239)	8. b;(p. 237)	9. d;(p. 240)
10. a;(p. 237)	11. d;(p. 244)	12. b;(p. 236)
13. e;(p. 243)	14. a;(p. 244)	15. e;(p. 246)
16. e;(p. 246)	17. c;(p. 246)	18d. a;(p. 252)
19. e;(p. 249)	20. a;(p. 251)	

TRUE-FALSE

1. T;(p. 236)   2. F;(p. 236)   3. F;(p. 237)

4. F;(p. 238)   5. F;(p. 241)   6. F;(p. 240)

7. F;(p. 245)   8. F;(p. 246)   9. T;(p. 246)

10. T;(p. 250)   11. T;(p. 250)

CHAPTER 11.

Small-*n* Experimentation

Summary

I.   Large-*n* vs Small-*n* Experimentation
  A. Typical experiments use many subjects
     1. and they are called **large-*n* designs**
     2. unusual individual participants do not skew the results of large-*n* designs
  B. In **small-*n* designs**, a few participants are intensely analyzed.
     1. Small-*n* designs are commonly used by behaviorally-oriented psychologists and are often used to evaluate treatments designed to control undesired behavior.
     2. A **functional analysis** of the behavior is often performed before the treatment is administered, in an attempt to identify the antecedents and consequences of the target behavior.
II. Operant-Conditioning Designs
  A. **The AB design** is a common but invalid way to evaluate the effectiveness of a treatment
     1. *A* represents the baseline condition before treatment
     2. *B* is the condition after treatment
     3. This design is invalid because any change might be due to other, unknown factors that changed when the treatment was administered.
  B. **The ABA** or **Reversal Design**
     1. removes the treatment to determine if behavior returns to baseline levels.
     2. If behavior does return to baseline, the experimenter can conclude that the treatment was responsible for the effect.

C. **Alternating-Treatments Design** are used
  1. to compare the effects of 2 or more different treatments
  2. Rose (1978) used a *ACABCBC* design to investigate two different treatments (*B* and *C*) on hyperactivity of children.
D. **Multiple-Baseline Designs** can be used is there are strong carryover effects
  1. different participants or different target behaviors have baselines of different durations to determine if the target behaviors are related or independent.
E. **Changing-Criterion Designs** are used to strengthen desired behavior.
  1. The amount (intensity, duration) of the desired behavior that is necessary to produce a reward is gradually increased during a series of therapy sessions.
III. Clinical Psychology
  A. The case study is a small-*n* design often used in clinical psychology

KEY TERM MATCHING

1.

___ AB design

___ ABA design

___ alternating-treatments design

___ changing-criterion design

___ functional analysis

___ large-*n* design

___ multiple-baseline design

___ small-*n* design

a. determining the antecedent and consequences of a target behavior
b. increasing the amount of a desired behavior necessary for reward
c. many observations on a few subjects
d. many observations following an extended treatment
e. observation of behavior is made before and after a treatment is applied
f. small-n design that returns to baseline conditions after a treatment has been administered
g. small-*n* design used to assess different behaviors or different people
h. traditional between- and within-subjects experiments

PROGRAMMED REVIEW

1. The *n* in a small-*n* design refers to the number of _____ .

2. In an AB design, A represents the _____ condition and B represents the condition after the _____ variable had been introduced.

3. Carefully noting the antecedents and consequences of a target behavior prior to using a treatment is called _____ _____ .

4. In the AB design the researcher cannot conclusively establish that the variable introduced during the B phase caused the change in behavior, because there is a _____ inherent in this design.

5. Another name for the ABA design is the _____ design.

6. In the ABA design during the second A phase the _____ variable is no longer applied, but the _____ _____ is still recorded.

7. If the behavior during the second A phase of an ABA design, returns to the level of the first A phase, then we can conclude that the _____ variable applied during the _____ phase actually effected the change.

8. In the study by Hart et al. during the B phase the teacher attempted to _____ the crying behavior by not paying attention, while _____ Bill whenever he behaved in an appropriate manner.

9. In the Hart et al, study, the number of crying episodes _____ during the second _____ phase and _____ during both _____ phases.

10. Small-*n* designs often include _____ effects that prohibit the reversal design.

11. A _____ - _____ design might be used to evaluate 2 or more treatments.

12. In Rose's (1978) experiment on the effects of artificial food colors on hyperactivity, the B and C phases include different _____ variables but the same _____ variable is employed in both phases.

13. A _____ - _____ is used when the behavioral requirement for a reward is altered during the course of therapy.

14. Because Nissen's (1988) study of memory dysfunction in a patient with multiple personality disorder is based on a single subject, it is an example of a _____ _____ .

15. Nissen found that faces shown to one personality (would be, would not be) _____ recognized by another personality.

16. Nissen found that words judged as to their pleasantness by one personality, (would be, would not be) _____ used in a word completion task by another personality, at a greater than chance rate.

EXPERIMENTAL PROJECT

Imagine that you have a good friend, who is otherwise a fine person, but who has one annoying habit that bothers you. (You can select your friend's bad habit) Moreover, you believe that your friend would be better off socially and be happier, if he/she would only smile more.

Decide on a 'treatment' that will reduce the frequency of the bad habit, and a second 'treatment' that is likely to increase your friend's smiling behavior. Then figure out a way, using the concepts in this chapter, to determine whether your treatments would be effective.

EXPERIMENTAL DILEMMA

Waldo, a mischievous little fellow, liked to play 'hide and seek'. Even when nobody else wanted to play with him he would hide in the strangest places, much to the distress and irritation of his parents. Waldo's Mom, who once had a course in developmental psychology, decided that enough was enough, and spray-painted Waldo a brilliant lilac color, so that he would be easier to find. And Waldo stopped hiding! Mom decided that her 'treatment' had cured Waldo's problem. Do you agree with Mom? What kind of a design did she use? What else might have been responsible for the change in Waldo's behavior?

MULTIPLE CHOICE

1. The *n* in small-*n* designs refers to the number of
   a. dependent variables.
   b. independent variables.
   c. measurements.
   d. participants.

2. In small-*n* designs, usually _____ observations are made of _____ participants.
   a. few; few
   b. few; many
   c. many; few
   d. many; many

3. Carefully noting the antecedents and consequences of a target behavior is called
   _____ _____ and should be done _____ the administration
   of the treatment.
   a. dysfunctional analysis; before
   b. dysfunctional analysis; after
   c. functional analysis; before
   d. functional analysis; after

4. In an ABA design, A refers to _____ and B refers to _____.
   a. baseline; experimental treatment
   b. baseline; dependent variable
   c. experimental treatment; baseline
   d. experimental treatment; dependent variable

5. When using an AB design in the clinical treatment of maladaptive behavior, the
   first step is to:
   a. extinguish the maladaptive behavior.
   b. reinforce adaptive behaviors.
   c. obtain a baseline of the maladaptive behavior.
   d. both a and b

6. An AB design is a poor design because
   a. there may be a confounding of uncontrolled factors and level of the
      independent variable.
   b. it is only appropriate to use with a small-n design.
   c. experimenter bias usually plays a role.
   d. it is impossible to obtain a stable baseline measure with only a single
      baseline phase.
   e. both b and c

7. The ABA design
   a. is a small-n design.
   b. is a between-subjects design.
   c. is also called a reversal design.
   d. all of the above
   e. both a and c

8. Which of the following is considered the more optimum small-n design?
   a. AB designs
   b. ABA designs
   c. ABC designs
   d. ABB designs

9. A common extension of the reversal design that is used when there are more then two treatments, and which provided multiple baseline periods is called
   a. alternating-treatments design
   b. cumulative-treatments design
   c. sequential-treatments design
   d. multiple-baseline design

10. The multiple-baseline design is useful when
    a. there are several treatments to be compared
    b. there are several different target behaviors
    c. There are several different people under observation
    d. a and b
    e. a and c
    f. b and c

11. If the treatment is likely to have strong carry-over effects, the use of a _____ design is recommended.
    a. alternating-treatments
    b. changing-criterion
    c. multiple-baseline
    d. reversal

12. Rose's study of the effects of oatmeal cookies and artificial food coloring on hyperactivity showed that hyperactivity was highest
    a. with the K-P diet used in the A phase.
    b. with oatmeal cookies, both colored and uncolored.
    c. with artificially colored oatmeal cookies.
    d. with artificially colored K-P diet.

13. Increasing the behavioral requirement that is necessary to earn a reward is an example of the _____ design
    a. changing-criterion
    b. ABCD
    c. multiple-baseline
    d. partial-reinforcement

14. Nissen, et al. (1988) showed that a patient with a multiple personality disorder could
    a. easily remember things shown to any of her other personalities.
    b. could only remember things shown to the same personality that was being tested.
    c. had better than chance recognition memory for faces shown to another personality.
    d. had a better than chance probability of using a word shown to another personality in a word completion task.

15. Nissen's study of memory dysfunction in multiple personality disorders was an example of
    a. an ABA design.
    b. a case study.
    c. operant-conditioning.
    d. time-lag design.

True-False

____ 1. Typically in small-n research, a small number of observations are made on many participants.

____ 2. Small-n research is used when Mill's joint method of agreement and difference is not appropriate.

____ 3. The AB design is a very poor small-n design because the researcher cannot be sure the obtained effect is due to the independent variable.

____ 4. The advantage of the ABA design over the AB design is that in the ABA design the second A phase allows the researcher to determine whether the behavior will return to baseline levels when the experimental treatment is no longer applied.

____ 5. In a patient with a multiple personality disorder, the more ambiguous the memory task, the more likely it is that one personality will have access to information presented to another personality.

ESSAY QUESTIONS

1. Why is an ABA design preferable to an AB design? What conclusions can you draw from an ABA design that you cannot draw from an AB design?

2. Why is it a good idea to conduct functional analysis of target behavior before conducting small-n experimentation?

3. Why is a multiple-baseline design strongly recommended for treatments with strong carry-over effects?

ANSWERS

KEY TERM MATCHING

1. e. f. d, b, a, h, g, c

PROGRAMMED REVIEW

1. participants; (p. 260)
2. baseline, independent; (p. 262)
3. functional analysis; (p. 266)
4. confounding; (p. 262)
5. reversal; (p. 262)
6. independent, target behavior; (p. 262)
7. independent, B; (p. 262)
8. extinguish, reward; (p. 263)
9. decreased, increased, baseline; (p. 263)
10. carryover; (p. 265)
11. alternating-treatments; (p. 265)
12. independent, dependent; (p. 265)
13. changing criterion; (p. 270)
14. case study; (p. 271)
15. would be; (p. 272)
16. would not be; (p. 272)

MULTIPLE CHOICE

1. d; (p. P)
2. c; (p. 260)
3. c; (p. 266)
4. a; (p. 262)
5. c; (p. 261)
6. a; (p. 262)
7. e; (p. 262)
8. b; (p. 262)
9. a; (p. 265)
10. e; (p. 267)
11. c; (p. 269)
12. c; (p. 265)
13. a; (p. 270)
14. c; (p. 272)
15. b; (p. 271)

True-False

1. F; (p. 260)　　　2. F; (p. 262)　　　3. T; (p. 262)

4. T; (p. 262)　　　5. F; (p. 273)

CHAPTER 12.

Quasi-Experimentation

SUMMARY

I. Internal Validity in Quasi-Experiments

  A. **Quasi-experiments** include "independent" variables that are selected rather than manipulated. This means that the internal validity is suspect in quasi-experiments.

  B. Natural Treatments are often studied with an *AB* design; behavior before and after some naturally occurring event is compared.

    1. It is dangerous to attribute behavioral changes to the natural treatment because:

      a. The treatment is not under the experimenter's control

      b. Most natural treatments have long term carryover effects

      c. **Maturation** - changes that occur in subjects during the time of the study.

      d. **History** - other changes in the world unrelated to the natural treatment can affect the observed behavior.

    2. Attempts to minimize the effects of maturation and history include adding a **nonequivalent control group** that is matched to the experimental group ex post facto. This procedure is suspect because of a possible **selection bias** in forming the control group

  C. **One-Shot Case Study**

    1. Behavior is observed following a long-term treatment. This is similar to the *AB* design.

    2. Deviant-case analysis is one way to obtain a control group in case-study research

  D. **Interrupted-Time-Series Design**

1. Many observations are made both before and after a naturally occurring treatment.

2. Marked behavioral changes following the treatment may be due to the treatment, but other interpretations are possible.

3. **Mortality** - the loss of subjects over time - is a particular threat to the internal validity of long-term interrupted time series research.

4. The internal validity of interrupted-time-series designs can be improved by using an untreated nonequivalent control group or using several dependent variables

II. Designs Employing Subject-Variables

  A. Subject-variables

    1. are measurable characteristics of people such as sex, age, attractiveness, etc.

    2. cannot be manipulated by the experimenter; subjects are *selected* to be in various groups because of these characteristics.

    3. Behavioral differences cannot be said to have been caused by different levels of a subject-variable. The relationship is correlational.

  B. Matching subjects on other relevant variables may increase the interval validity of studies employing subject-variables. But there are problems:

    1. Matching is difficult and expensive.

    2. Matching can severely reduce the sample size.

    3. Interactions among matched variables may confound the results.

      a. Brazelton demonstrated a synergistic interaction among matching variables used in a study of neonate behavior. **Synergism** refers to a more than additive effect of combining two variables.

    4. Matching procedures can lead to **regression artifacts**. Subjects selected because of their extreme scores on a matching variable (to match with people in another group) are likely to score closer to their own group mean when they are retested.

  C. Age as a Variable

    1. Age is an important and popular variable in development psychology.

    2. Research designs for studying age:

      a. the **cross-sectional method** - subjects of various ages are selected to form the experimental groups

        (1) but age is confounded with generation of birth; people of

different ages are born into different social environments

b. the **longitudinal method** - the same subjects are measured at various ages.

    (1) but age is confounded with the state of the world. Not only is the subject older, but also the world has changed from one testing to another.

c. the **time lag design** - people born in different years are tested when they reach the same age. This procedure allows the time of testing to be evaluated while holding age constant.

d. the **cross-sequential design** tests two or more age groups at two or more time periods. This allows the investigator to determine the effects of most of the potential confoundings.

KEY TERM MATCHING

1.

___ cross-sectional method

___ cross-sequential design

___ interrupted-time-series design

___ longitudinal method

___ one-shot case study

___ time-lag design

a. AB design for a natural treatment
b. compares people born in different years when they reach a specific age
c. people born in a particular year are measured at several specific ages
d. people born in different years are tested at two or more specific ages
e. people of different ages are compared
f. several measurements both before and after a natural treatment

2.

___ history

___ interaction

___ matching

___ maturation

___ mortality

___ nonequivalent control group

___ quasi-experiment

___ regression artifact

___ subject variable

___ synergism

a. attempt to form a comparison group in quasi-experiments

b. changes in subjects over time that confound the interpretation of a natural treatment

c. comparison subjects that are matched to subjects who have been exposed to a natural treatment

d. distortion resulting from statistical regression to the mean

e. experiments that include one or more uncontrolled variables

f. interaction in which the combined effects of two variables exceed the sum of their individual effects

g. measurable characteristic on which people differ

h. possible problem associated with matching

i. the effect of one independent variable depends of the level of a second independent variable

j. uncontrolled changes in a setting that confound the interpretation of a natural treatment

PROGRAMMED REVIEW

1. Quasi-experiments allow the researcher to examine variables that would be _____ to manipulate directly.

2. Most quasi-experiments involving naturally occurring events are similar in structure to small-n _____ designs.

3.   Quasi-experiments of the general form observation-treatment-observation are not true reversal designs because
(a)_____
_____ and
(b)_____
_____

4.   Two threats to internal validity with naturally occurring treatments are the _____ of the participant and any changes in the _____ that occur over time.

5.   In a nonequivalent control group design the experimenter attempts to _____ two groups after one group has received some treatments.

6.   The primary threat to internal validity associated with the one-shot case study is the lack of a _____ _____ .

7.   In a typical case study the researcher gains control by increasing the _____ of observations.

8.   In long-term time series studies the participants may be unavailable late in the study, a confounding factor that is called _____ . This confounding would lead to a special form of _____ bias.

9.   The difficulties of the interrupted-time-series design are magnified when the _____ of the treatment is delayed or masked by other variables.

10. Sex, height, and IQ are all _____ variables.

11. Designs employing subject variables essentially produce _____ between variables.

12. A problem inherent in studies employing subject variables is that whatever results are obtained may be caused by _____ variables.

13. One way to avoid confounding with subject variables is _____ .

14. Matching often greatly reduces _____ size.

15. Synergism of two variables means that the two variables do not have _____ effects but rather they _____ .

16. Matching may lead to _____ artifacts.

17. In a _____ design the same participantt is tested repeatedly over a long time period.

18. In a _____-_____ design the researcher selects children from different ages and observes their behavior on one occasion.

19. Age is not a true _____ variable.

20. As an individual goes through life he maintains the same _____, or group of people born at approximately the same time period.

21. A time-lag design attempts to determine the effects of the time of _____ while holding _____ constant.

EXPERIMENTAL PROJECT

One "naturally occurring" event for college and university students is examinations. Hence these events represent an excellent opportunity to use a quasi-experimental approach to test a hypotheses. From studies of the effect of various schedules of reinforcement on behavior patterns, we know that there is often a post-response pause that follows reinforcement when the organism is on a partial reinforcement schedule. It has been suggested that a similar `pause' occurs following major examinations. (Perhaps you have experienced this firsthand.)

To study this phenomenon, you will need to select one or two persons who will agree to allow you to monitor their study behavior. If you use a single subject, then record (or ask the person to record) the number of hours spent studying over a two-week period that contains an examination approximately mid-way through the observation period. If you use two persons, then for the second person record study behaviors during a two-week period in which no-examinations occur.

Before you rush out and carry out this project there are several things you will need to consider. Is the fact that you are monitoring the person's behavior likely to change the person's behavior? If you use two persons, how are you going to match these individuals? What possible threats to internal validity are inherent in this design? External validity?

Once you collect the data, are you tempted to say that having the exam finished caused the person to decrease their rate of study behavior? If not, how would you go about collecting data that would allow you to infer a causal relation?

EXPERIMENTAL DILEMMAS

1. As part of an investigation of the effects of biorhythms on various physical and psychological abilities a researcher decided to measure absolute threshold early in

the morning and then again late at night. Each morning the researcher went to his laboratory at 6:00 a.m. and tested his subjects' absolute threshold, using the method of limits to determine the absolute threshold for detecting a 400 Hz tone embedded in white noise. At night the subjects reported to the University Sleep Lab to be tested. The Sleep Lab was equipped with a microcomputer which make it easy to test the subjects absolute threshold using the staircase method. As in the morning session, the subject's task was to detect the presence of a 400 Hz tone embedded in white noise.

The results showed that, on average, the subjects' absolute threshold was lower in the morning than in the evening. That is, the absolute threshold stimulus intensity was lower in the morning than in the evening. The researcher concluded that time of day has an affect upon auditory absolute threshold, with people being more sensitive in the morning than in the afternoon.

Do you agree or disagree with this conclusion? Why or why not?

2.   A psychologist interested in the effect of personality traits upon various psychological abilities decided to test whether introverts or extroverts are more sensitive to external stimulation. His hypothesis was that introverts, who are basically quiet, shy people, would be more sensitive to the external world than would extroverts, who he thought would be more sensitive to internal stimulation. To test this hypothesis he decided to see which group of subjects would be better able to detect a very faint amount of pressure applied to the back of the hand.

Ten introverts and 10 extroverts were selected on the basis of a personality test. All subjects were paid for their participation. Subjects were each tested individually by the same experimenter. Subjects were blindfolded and then given 200 trials. On half of the trials, a very faint amount of pressure was applied to the back of the subjects hand by means of a mechanical device. The amount of pressure was constant for all subjects. On the remaining trials no pressure was applied to the subjects hand. All subjects were right handed, and only the right hand was used in the experiment. Finally, a different random order of pressure trials and no pressure trials was used for each subject. Subjects were not told how many trials there would be, only that there would be "a lot." No subject was told what percentage of trials would be "touch" trials.

Results showed that, averaged across subject, the extroverts responded correctly on 85% of the touch trials and were incorrect on 15% of these trials. Introverts, however were only correct on 70% of the touch trials, making 30% errors on these trials. These differences between groups were reliable.

The research concluded that these results indicated that extroverts were more sensitive than introverts, since they were correct on more of the touch trials (85% versus 70%). Since this was exactly the opposite of what he had predicted he decided that his hypothesis needed to be revised.

Do you agree with this conclusion? Why or why not? How would you design an experiment to test this hypothesis?

3. A researcher submitted the following work to a journal for publication. Twenty second graders were selected to participate in a remedial reading program based on scores obtained on a general reading skills test given to all children in the school system. The students were chosen because they did not perform as well as their classmates in general reading skills, and it was hoped that the program would improve their reading ability. The program involved individual sessions with a special instructor three hours a week for six weeks. At the end of this period, the test was readministered to the students in the program. Scores were compared with those of children of similar ability from another grammar school in the area who took the test again at the same point in the school year as the children in the remedial program. The results showed no difference between scores for students who had participated in the remedial program and those who had not. Although the researcher wanted to conclude that the program had been ineffective, a reviewer argued that the results could have been due to regression artifacts. Do you agree with the reviewer? Why or why not?

MULTIPLE CHOICE

1. Quasi-experiments in the general form observation-treatment-observation cannot be true reversal designs because
   a. most natural treatments have long-term carry-over effects.
   b. there is no control condition.
   c. the variables are generally confounded.
   d. all of the above
2. One way to obtain a "control" group or condition in case-study research is to
   a. employ a time-series design.
   b. employ a deviant-case analysis.
   c. replicate the research in a controlled laboratory experiment.
   d. randomly assign subjects to either the case-study condition or the control condition.

3. In a time-series analysis we are interested in
    a. consistent patterns of responding across the individuals' life span.
    b. separating changes in behavior that are due to maturation from changes that are due to treatment effects.
    c. determining the relative effect of a treatment as a function of when the treatment was introduced.
    d. changes following introduction of the treatment.

4. One way to increase internal validity in case study research is to use
    a. deviant case analysis.
    b. nonequivalent control groups.
    c. multiple dependent variables.
    d. all of the above

5. Which of the following is not a subject variable?
    a. sex of individual
    b. political affiliation
    c. weight
    d. age
    e. all of the above are subject variables

6. Which of the following represents a quasi-experimental research project?
    a. Memory performance is compared between a group of subjects who study material for 10 minutes versus a group who studies for 20 minutes.
    b. Perception of light flashes is compared between subjects who are dark-adapted and those who are not.
    c. SAT scores are compared for students in private and public schools.
    d. Arousal level is measured as a function of type of music presented to subjects.

7. Which of the following is true concerning quasi-experimental designs?
    a. they are less powerful than observational studies
    b. they often include subject variables
    c. they involve careful manipulation of experimental variables
    d. they are rarely used in psychological research

8. Matching
    a. is used in quasi-experiments.
    b. is a way of avoiding confounding of subject variables.
    c. introduces the possibility of regression artifacts.
    d. all of the above

9. If a researcher wants to use a research design that employs subject variables, then that researcher will
   a. manipulate the subject variable holding other factors constant.
   b. select subjects who have the chosen characteristics in some varying degree.
   c. select a behavior to measure that will not vary with the subject variable.
   d. both b and c

10. In designs that employ subject variables, matching refers to
    a. matching subjects on the subject variables.
    b. matching subjects on the behavioral task that is measured.
    c. matching subjects on the variables that may be confounded with the subject variable.
    d. matching subjects on variables that are known to be confounded with the behavioral task.

11. The phenomenon of regression to the mean implies that if two abnormally tall parents have a child, the child's adult height will likely be
    a. shorter than the mean of the parents' heights.
    b. taller than the mean of the parents' heights.
    c. close to the mean of the parents' heights.
    d. either a or c

12. A synergistic relationship among two variables indicates that
    a. the two variables interact.
    b. the two variables are correlated.
    c. the two variables are confounded.
    d. both a and c

13. Given that age is a subject variable,
    a. it may be directly manipulated in an experimental design.
    b. it is easy to attribute causation to the age factor as opposed to any other factor in an experimental design.
    c. it is examined largely in correlational studies rather than in experimental designs.
    d. it may only be treated as a control variable in developmental research.

14. A researcher interested in the long-term effects of nuclear wastes monitors the health of 15 families living near a waste disposal site. The researcher records any instance of physical or mental illness reported by the families over a period of 10 years. This sort of study is called a _____ design.
    a. cross-sectional
    b. cross-sequential
    c. longitudinal
    d. time-lag

15. In a longitudinal design
    a. the confoundings inherent in cross-sectional designs are avoided.
    b. results may be produced by historical events occurring during the course of the study.
    c. the same group of subjects are repeatedly tested as they grow older.
    d. all of the above

16. Cross-sectional research designs
    a. allow for causal inferences concerning the effects of subject variables.
    b. confound age with other subject variables of interest.
    c. are much more difficult to run than longitudinal studies.
    d. all of the above

TRUE-FALSE

____ 1. Ex post facto analysis involving more than one dependent variable may be interpreted in a causal fashion.

____ 2. Quasi-experiments of the general form observation-treatment-observation can best be considered a reversal, or ABA design.

____ 3. Two threats to internal validity with naturally occurring treatments are the history of the subject and changes in the subject that occur over time.

____ 4. In a nonequivalent control group, matching is attempted after the occurrence of the treatment.

____ 5. An interrupted-time-series design is the best design that can be used when the size of the effect of the treatment is expected to be delayed for some period.

____ 6. Ability to recall dreams is an example of a subject variable.

____ 7. When manipulating a subject variable it is important to hold all other factors constant.

____ 8. Studies involving subject variables essentially produce correlations between variables.

____ 9. Matching subjects on relevant variables avoids problems caused by confounding.

____ 10. Regression procedures often lead to matching artifacts.

____ 11. In a synergistic relationship the two variables exhibit additive effects.

____ 12. Matching often reduces the size of the sample on which observations are made.

____ 13. Matched variables are rarely under direct control.

____ 14. Regression to the mean refers to the phenomenon whereby if people who receive extreme scores on some characteristic are retested, their second scores tend to be closer to the group mean than were their first scores.

____ 15. In a cross-sectional research design, the same subjects are repeatedly tested over the course of several years.

____ 16. Longitudinal and cross-sectional studies can produce different results due to the fact that age may be confounded with other factors in cross-sectional designs.

____ 17. The confounding inherent in cross-sequential designs is eliminated in longitudinal studies.

____ 18. Longitudinal designs tend to confound age with other subject variables.

____ 19. Time-lag designs determine the effects of time of testing while holding age constant.

____ 20. Cross-sequential designs include both longitudinal and cross-sectional components.

ESSAY QUESTIONS

1. Why is an ABA design preferable to an AB design? What conclusions can you draw from an ABA design that you cannot draw from an AB design?

2. In what sense is it meaningful to compare interpreting a case history and doing detective work?

3. Describe briefly the ways in which the internal validity of case studies may be increased.

4. Describe briefly problems associated with the use of age as a subject variable. How might these problems be avoided?

5. What is a cross-sequential design? How is it an improvement over other research designs employing subject variables?

ANSWERS

KEY TERM MATCHING
1. e, d, f, c, a, b

2. j, i, a, b, h, c, e, d, g, f

PROGRAMMED REVIEW
1. impossible; (p. 278)
2. experimental; (p. 278)
3. treatment is not removed, treatment likely to have carryover effects; (p. 278)
4. maturation, setting; (p. 278)
5. match; (p. 279)
6. control condition; (p. 279)
7. number; (p. 280)
8. mortality, selection; (p. 283)
9. effect; (p. 283)
10. subject; (p. 285)
11. confounding; (p. 286)
12. correlations; (p. 286)
13. matching; (p. 287)
14. sample; (p. 288)
15. additive, interactive; (p. 288)
16. regression; (p. 288)
17. longitudinal; (p. 291)
18. cross-sectional; (p. 291)
19. independent; (p. 291)
20. cohorts; (p. 291)
21. testing, age; (p. 291)

MULTIPLE CHOICE

1. b; (p. 278)   2. c; (p. 280)   3. d; (p. 282)

4. d; (p. 283)   5. e; (p. 285)   6. x; (p. 286)

7. b; (p. 286)   8. d; (p. 287)   9. b; (p. 286)

10. c; (p. 287)   11. a; (p. 288)   12. a; (p. 288)

13. c; (p. 291)   14. c; (p. 291)   15. d; (p. 291)

16. b; (p. 291)

TRUE-FALSE

1. F; (p. 278)   2. F; (p. 278)   3. T; (p. 278)

4. T; (p. 279)   5. T; (p. 283)   6. T; (p. 285)

7. F; (p. 286)   8. T; (p. 286)   9. F; (p. 287)

10. F; (p. 288)   11. F; (p. 288)   12. T; (p. 288)

13. T; (p. 288)   14. T; (p. 288)   15. F; (p. 291)

16. T; (p. 291)   17. T; (p. 292)   18. T; (p. 291)

19. T; (p. 291)   20. T; (p. 292)

Chapter 13.
Interpreting the Results of Research

SUMMARY
I.   Interpreting Specific Results
    A.   The Problem of Scale-Attenuation
        1.   **Scale-Attenuation effects** include
            a.   **Ceiling effects** occur when performance measures cluster near the upper end of the scale, suggesting that true performance may exceed the upper limits of the measurement scale.
            b.   **Floor effects** occur when performance measures cluster near the lower end of the scale, suggesting that true performance may be lower than the lower limits of the measurement scale.
        2.   Scale-attenuation distorts the results, and may suggest the presence of an interaction when there is none.
        3.   Scarborough's experiment on the difference between visual and auditory presentation on retention was used to illustrate scale-attenuation effects.
        4.   Possible scale-attenuation effects may be revealed by pilot research which may suggest that the difficulty of the experimental task should be increased (for ceiling effects) or reduced (for floor effects).
    B.   **Regression Artifacts**
        1.   arise from the statistical phenomenon called **regression to the mean**.
            a.   All measurements include some amount of random error.
            b.   When a group of people are measured, the extreme scores are likely to be high or low in part because of this measurement error.

        c.   If these people were measured again, the pattern of random error would be different. This means that the new scores of the people who made extreme scores on the first test would likely be closer to the group mean on the second test. The extreme scorers have *regressed toward the mean.*

    2.   Regression artifacts are an important threat to the internal validity of quasi-experiments when the nonequivalent control groups are formed on the basis of matching participants on the basis of subject variables.

    3.   This problem is particularly dangerous when control participants with extreme scores are selected to match people from a group with a different mean.

    4.   Cicirelli and Granger's evaluation of the Head Start Program was considered with respect to regression artifacts.

    5.   Whenever possible, participants should be randomly assigned to the treatment conditions.

II.   Interpreting Patterns of Research

    A.   Reliability and Replication

        1.   **Test reliability** refers to consistency of measurements.

        2.   **Experimental reliability** refers to the consistency of results over **replications.**

            a.   Types of replication

                (1)   **Direct replication** refers to repeating an experiment as closely as possible to the original.

                (2)   **Systematic replication** deliberately modifies many factors believed to be irrelevant to the original results.

                (3)   **Conceptual replication** attempts to replicate a finding in an entirely different way, by using a different operational definition of the concept.

            b.   As we progress from direct to conceptual replication, we extend the external validity of the results.

            c.   Luchin's **Einstellung** (or set) experiments were considered with respect to experimental reliability.

    B.   **Converging Operations**

        1.   are a set of two or more operations the eliminate alternative concepts that might explain a set of experimental results.

2. Examples of research that used converging operations are
   a. the Stroop effect in which converging operations were used to distinguish between perceptual and response sources of interference in naming the color of ink used to spell another color name.
   b. research on **personal space** in which the concept was defined by very different operational definitions.

KEY TERM MATCHING

1.

____ conceptual replication

____ converging operations

____ direct replication

____ regression artifact

____ scale-attenuation effect

____ systematic replication

a. a threat to internal validity in matched-groups quasi-experiments
b. deliberately changing factors believed to be irrelevant
c. floor and ceiling effects
d. independent procedures that eliminate alternate explanations
e. redoing an experiment under the original conditions
f. using new operational definitions

2.

____ Einstellung

____ experimental reliability

____ personal space

____ regression to the mean

____ Stroop effect

____ test reliability

a. area surrounding a person outside of which another person is not threatening
b. consistency of measures
c. difficulty in naming to color of ink used to write another color name
d. established through replication
e. extreme scorers on a test tend to score closer to the group average in a second test.
f. response set

PROGRAMMED REVIEW

1. Performance levels near either to the top or the bottom of the scale of the dependent variable are called _____-_____ effects.

2. _____ effects are observed when performance is nearly perfect, and _____ effects are observed when performance is almost nonexistent.

3. Scarborough found that recall was higher in the _____ presentation condition than in the _____ presentation condition.

4. Scarborough's data showed evidence of a _____ effect at the zero-second retention interval.

5. Researchers usually test small groups of _____ participants to determine whether ceiling or floor effects are going to be a problem in their research.

6. If a scale-attenuation problem exists, then one way to avoid this problem is to change the _____ of the task.

7. If people are given two successive tasks, and we find that those who scored high in test 1 tended to score somewhat lower on test 2, this would represent a statistical _____ to the _____.

8. Regression artifacts occur because all psychological measurements are subject to a certain amount of _____.

9. In the Westinghouse-Ohio study, the two samples of children probably came from different _____.

10. The best method for eliminating confounding factors is _____ _____ of participants to conditions.

11. Two key factors for ensuring reliability are a _____ number of observations and a _____ result.

12. An unreliable test is also an _____ test.

13. Many experimental psychologists find _____ reliability more convincing than statistical reliability.

14. In Luchin's water-jar problem, the (experimental/control) _____ group received all 11 of the problems to be solved.

15. In a _____ _____, an experiment is repeated as closely as possible, and with as few changes as possible in the method.

16. In a _____ replication, many factors that the investigator considers irrelevant to the phenomenon of interest are changed in the replication.

17. _____ _____ are a set of two or more operations that eliminate alternative concepts that might explain a set of experimental results.

18. In a(n) _____ task, participants are required to name the color of ink that a word is printed in.

19. The Stroop effect is an (increase/decrease) _____ in the time needed to name the color of the ink used to spell the name of a different color.

20. By using converging operations, Egeth, Blecker and Kamlet (1969) showed that the Stroop effect is due to _____ _____ and not to _____ _____ .

21. In Kinzel's (1970) study on personal space, the dependent variable was

_____ .

22. Barefoot, Hoople and McClay (1792) found that _____ people stopped to drink water when the experimenter sat close to the fountain than when he sat far from the fountain.

EXPERIMENTAL PROJECT

Luchins's (1942) water-jar problems have been studied extensively and Luchins's original results have been found to be highly reliable. In this project you can determine whether the same results would be obtained under conditions in which the problem solver is under time pressure. Specifically, will the group of subjects who write "Don't be blind" prior to problem 7 (see text page 237) show less of an Einstellung effect than the experimental group when they are trying to solve the problem as rapidly as possible? To test this hypothesis conduct a replication of Luchins' original demonstration, as described on pages 237-238 of the text. Tell half of your subjects that you are going to time their problem solving, and that they should work as quickly as possible. Do not mention this to the remaining subjects.

Did the time-pressure subjects show the same pattern of results as the no time-pressure group? What do these results indicate about the generality of Luchins' results?

EXPERIMENTAL DILEMMA

A researcher working for the Defense Department wanted to determine whether pilots or air traffic controllers were more affected by environmental stress. The researcher selected a task known as a speech shadowing task to answer this question. In a speech shadowing task two different messages are presented to the subjects, one in each ear (i.e., a dichotic message) and the subjects' task is to repeat aloud (shadow) the message presented in one ear.

Ten pilots and 10 air traffic controllers were selected for the experiment. The subjects were matched on age, years in their respective occupations, and sex. Each group of subjects shadowed a dichotic message under two conditions, a high stress condition and a low stress condition. Subjects received 20 trials under each condition in an ABBA design. Each trial consists of the presentation of five different items to both the attended and the unattended ear. The subjects' task is to shadow one message (the attended message), and when the message is completed to try and recall the items presented to the unattended ear. Items are presented at the rate of one item pair per second. The assignment of items to the unattended and attended ear is completely counterbalanced across subjects and conditions.

The dependent variable is the number of items recalled from the nonattended ear. The mean number of items recalled in each condition was as follows:

Participants	Stress Condition	
	Low Stress	High Stress
Pilots	97%	80%
Copilots	98%	94%

Because there was an interaction effect the researcher concluded that the pilots were more affected by stress than were the controllers, although this difference was only present in the high stress condition. Under low stress conditions the two groups were equally affected by stress.

Do you agree or disagree with this conclusion? Why or why not? How would you design an experiment to test whether pilots or controllers are more affected by stress?

MULTIPLE CHOICE

1. Scale attenuation effects are observed when
   a. subjects fail to show any savings from one learning trial to the next.
   b. performance is virtually perfect or virtually nonexistent.
   c. recognition performance is superior to recall performance.
   d. recency effects are larger than primary effects.

2. Scarborough (1972) could not draw any conclusions about differential forgetting in his auditory and visual retention presentation conditions because
   a. performance in the auditory and visual presentation conditions was equivalent across all retention intervals.
   b. performance was virtually perfect in all conditions at the zero retention interval.
   c. performance was poorer in the auditory than in the visual presentation condition at the longer retention intervals.
   d. performance was poorer in the visual than in the auditory presentation at the longer retention intervals.

3. Which of the following statements best summarizes the problem of scale attenuation effects?
   a. There is no such thing as perfectly good or perfectly bad performance.
   b. The size of the intervals of a dependent measure are unequal when you approach the extreme ends of the scale.
   c. It is impossible to determine whether there are differences among experimental conditions when performance is polarized at either the high or low end of the scale of the dependent measure.
   d. Most of the dependent measures used to study memory are relatively unconstrained and thus allow for easy interpretation of performance levels.

4. One might reduce problems of ceiling and floor effects by
   a. avoiding the use of tasks that are too easy.
   b. avoiding the use of tasks that are too difficult.
   c. testing pilot subjects to make sure that performance on a task will not be near the extremes of the scale.
   d. all of the above

5. Statistical regression to the mean refers to the fact that
   a. when people are tested twice, those with high scores on test 1 tend to have scores that are closer to the group mean on test 2.
   b. in psychology most test scores tend to fall close to the mean, with few very deviant scores.
   c. in an experiment employing repeated tests, subjects who perform poorly on the early test(s) will tend to do better on the later test(s).
   d. both a and c

6. Quasi-experimental designs are particularly susceptible to bias due to measurement error because
    a. there are no control variables.
    b. subjects are not randomly assigned to groups.
    c. the experimental and control groups are not matched prior to the introduction of the independent variable.
    d. all of the above

7. Two students take a History exam. The first student has an A average but makes a C on the test whereas the second student who had a D average makes an A on the exam. Assuming that these discrepancies are due to measurement error, it is likely that the first student will make a(n) _____ and the second student will make a(n) _____ on the next exam.
    a. C; A
    b. A; C
    c. C; C
    d. C; B

8. The reliability of a test refers to
    a. whether the test measures what it is intended to measure.
    b. how well the test can predict future performance.
    c. how stable scores are across testings of the same subjects.
    d. how stable scores are across different groups.

9. The basic issue regarding reliability of experimental results is:
    a. whether we can draw a conclusion regarding a causal relation between the independent and dependent variables.
    b. if the experiment were repeated would the results be the same as were found the first time.
    c. whether the conclusions are warranted, given the design of the experiment.
    d. the presence or absence of possible confounding factors.

10. *Einstellung* is the German word for _____.
    a. problem
    b. experimentation
    c. reactivity
    d. set

11. In a _____ we replicate a phenomenon or concept, but in a way that differs from the original demonstration.
    a. systematic replication
    b. paradigmatic replication
    c. conceptual replication
    d. indirect replication

12. Converging operations
    a. are a set of two or more operations used to eliminate alternative explanations for a set of experimental results.
    b. provide more than one way of arriving at an experimental conclusion.
    c. allow psychologists to distinguish between two competing explanations of an effect.
    d. all of the above

13. Which of the following is true?
    a. Converging operations are useful in validating mental constructs.
    b. Converging operations are experimental operations that produce different results.
    c. Converging operations are a set of two or more operational definitions.
    d. both a and c.

14. The Stroop effect is a phenomenon in which the time required to name the color of the ink a word is printed in _____ when the word is the name of a color other than the ink as opposed to a neutral word.
    a. increases
    b. decreases
    c. remains constant
    d. increases for warm colors and decreases for cool colors

15. The results of the Egeth, Blecker and Kamlet (1969) experiment indicate that the Stroop effect has its influence on the _____ portion of the task.
    a. perceptual
    b. input
    c. inhibition
    d. response

16. The most important reason for a psychologist to use converging operations is to
    a. support inferences about processes that cannot be directly inferred.
    b. replicate an experimental finding to ensure its reliability.
    c. increase precision of the dependent variable.
    d. define a process in terms of its operations.

17. Prisoners were found to have larger personal space bubbles when they were classified as
    a. nonviolent.
    b. violent.
    c. depressed.
    d. homosexual.

18. Kinzel (1970) found that violent prisoners have
    a. larger personal space bubbles than nonviolent prisoners.
    b. smaller personal space bubbles than nonviolent prisoners.
    c. a larger personal space area in front than in behind.
    d. both a and c

19. In approaching a violent prisoner, you would be more likely to invade his personal space if you approached from the prisoner's
    a. left side.
    b. right side.
    c. front.
    d. rear.

True-False

1. Based on Scarborough's (1972) results we can conclude that forgetting is greater for auditory than for visual presentation.

2. There is no way to avoid ceiling and floor effects in psychological research; we just have to learn to interpret them carefully.

3. Scarborough (1972) concluded that his results indicated that the rate of forgetting is greater for information presented through the ears than through the eyes.

4. Scale attenuation effects can hide actual differences that may exist between experimental conditions.

5. Scale attenuation effects can be avoided by effectively manipulating task difficulty.

6. Regression to the mean is an experimental artifact.

7. Regression artifacts would never be a problem if measurement error could be eliminated completely.

8. Regression artifacts pose very few problems as long as subjects are drawn from different underlying populations.

9. Quasi-experimental designs are less susceptible to bias than true experiments because of regression to the mean.

10. If a test is reliable then we know that it measures what it was intended to measure.

11. Many psychologists find experimental reliability less convincing than statistical reliability.

12. A direct replication involves simply repeating an experiment as closely as possible with as few changes in the method as possible.

13. Kinzel (1970) found that violent prisoners have larger personal space "bubbles" than do nonviolent prisoners.

14. Converging operations are a set of two or more operations that suggest alternative explanations for an experimental result.

15. The general finding in the Stroop task is that the time required to name ink color decreases when the stimulus word is the name of a color other than the ink it is printed in.

16. Using converging operations, Egeth, Blecker and Kamlet (1969) showed that interference in the Stroop task was localized in the response system.

17. An experimenter can be satisfied that he or she has eliminated all alternative explanations of an experimental result if two converging operations have led to the same conclusion.

ESSAY QUESTIONS

1. Define and give an example of scale attenuation effects. Why are these effects problematic? How might a researcher avoid these problems?

2. What are converging operations? Describe how converging operations were used to discover the focus of the Stroop effect.

3. What is meant by regression to the mean? Can this problem arise only with a within-subject design or could it also arise when a between-subject design is employed? How might such regression effects affect the interpretation of experimental results?

ANSWERS

KEY TERM MATCHING

1. f, d, e, a, c, b   2. f, d, a, e, c, b

PROGRAMMED REVIEW

1. scale attenation; (p. 300)
2. ceiling, floor; (p. 300)
3. visual, auditory; (p. 302)
4. ceiling; (p. 302)
5. pilot; (p. 304)
6. difficulty; (p. 304)
7. regression, mean; (p. 305)
8. error; (p. 306)
9. populations; (p. 307)
10. random assignment; (p. 308)
11. large, repeatable; (p. 310)
12. invalid; (p. 310)
13. experimental; (p. 310)
14. experimental; (p. 311)
15. direct; (p. 312)
16. systematic; (p. 312)
17. converging operations; (p. 313)
18. Stroop; (p. 315)
19. increase; (p. 315)
20. response competition, perceptual inhibition; (p. 317)
21. proximity a prisoner would tolerate another person; (p. 318)
22. fewer; (p. 318)

MULTIPLE CHOICE

1. b; (p. 300)   2. b; (p. 303)   3. c; (p. 303)

4. d; (p. 304)   5. d; (p. 305)   6. b; (p. 307)

7. b; (p. 306)   8. c; (p. 310)   9. b; (p. 310)

10. d; (p. 311)   11. c; (p. 312)   12. d; (p. 313)

13. d; (p. 314)   14. a; (p. 315)   15. d; (p. 317)

16. a; (p. 315)   17. b; (p. 318)   18. a; (p. 319)

19. d; (p. 319)

TRUE-FALSE

1. F (p.303)   2. F; (p. 304)   3. F; (p.303)

4. T; (p. 303)   5. T; (p. 304)   6. F; (p. 305)

7. T; (p. 306)   8. F; (p. 306)   9. F; (p. 306)

10. F; (p. 309)   11. F; (p. 310)   12. T; (p. 312)

13. T; (p. 318)   14. T; (p. 313)   15. F; (p. 315)

16. T; (p. 317)   17. F; (p. 319)

CHAPTER 14.

Presenting Research Results

SUMMARY

I.   How to Write a Research Report
   A.   The self-correcting nature of science requires good data to be published
   B.   The *Publication Manual of the American Psychological Society* is the official arbiter of style for most journals in psychology
   C.   Format
      1.   The cover page of the copy manuscript contains
         a.   the title
         b.   author's name and affiliation
         c.   the **running head** which will appear at the top of each page in the published article
         d.   **short title** which identifies each page of the manuscript during editing.
      2.   The **abstract** appears on the second page
      3.   The full title appears on the third page, followed by the **introduction**
      4.   The **method** section immediately follows the introduction.
         a.   the use of side headings *Participants* , *Apparatus,* and *Procedure* will help guide the reader.
      5.   The **results** section immediately follows the method.
      6.   The **discussion** section immediately follows the results.
      7.   References begin on a separate page.

8. Any author notes or footnotes follow the references on a separate page.
9. Data tables mentioned in the results section follow the footnotes
10. Captions to figures appear next, followed by
11. Figures, one to each page, which complete the report.

D. Style
1. Transitions between sections should be smooth and straightforward.
2. Titles should be short, and mention the independent and dependent variables.
3. Avoid too much detail in the abstract.
4. The introduction should review relevant information and justify the present experiment to the reader
5. The method section should present enough information so that a reader could replicate your study.
6. The results section should state clearly what was found.
7. he discussion should relate your results to the question that motivated the research
8. The APA publication manual recommends that the writer
   a. use the precise word,
   b. avoid ambiguity,
   c. order the presentation of ideas, and
   d. consider the reader.
9. Finally,
   a. Use the present tense for the current experiment, and the past tense in review earlier work.
   b. Check for agreement between plural and collective nouns and their verbs.
   c. Don't overuse the passive or the active voice.

II. Publishing an Article
A. Articles are submitted to the editor of an appropriate journal
B. The editor sends the article to reviewers, who provide useful comments to the author.
C. The publication process usually takes over a year.

III. How to Give an Oral Presentation
A. Most oral presentations are limited to about 15 minutes.
B. The speaker should
1. avoid unnecessary detail
2. use appropriate visual aids
3. talk from an outline, rather than reading a paper.

KEY TERM MATCHING

1.

_____ abstract
_____ APA format
_____ copy manuscript
_____ discussion
_____ figures
_____ introduction
_____ materials
_____ method
_____ running head
_____ short title
_____ title

a.   between cover page and introduction
b.   gives enough detail to allow a replication of the experiment
c.   guide that standardizes order and context of an article
d.   heading that appears at the top of each page in published article
e.   heading that appears at the top of each page in the copy manuscript
f.   names independent and dependent variables
g.   only section of article that does not have a heading
h.   sideheading in method section
i.   the final page or pages of the copy manuscript
j.   version of the article prepared to facilitate editing
k.   where the results are interpreted

PROGRAMMED REVIEW

1.   In an APA-style report, the cover sheet includes

_____

_____

2.   Page two of a research report contains the _____.

3.   The title of a research project appears on the third page and immediately precedes the _____ section.

4.   Any published reports cited in a paper are listed in the _____.

5.   The biggest stylistic problem in most research reports is _____ from one section to the next.

6.   The _____ tense should be used in the Introduction and Method section and the _____ tense is generally acceptable for the Results and Discussion sections.

7.   Overuse of the _____ voice might be stuffy, while overuse of the _____ voice emphasizes the researcher rather than the study.

8. One is obliged to publish good data because of the _____ _____ nature of the scientific enterprise.

9. When giving an oral presentation, it is better to speak from an _____ rather than to _____ the paper.

ANSWERS

PROGRAMMED REVIEW

1. title, author, affiliation, running head, short title; (p. 324)
2. abstract; (p. 325)
3. introduction; (p. 325)
4. references; (p. 326)
5. transition; (p. 349)
6. past, present; (p. 351)
7. passive, active; (p. 351)
8. self-correcting; (p. 324)
9. outline, read; (p. 355)

Appendix A

Descriptive Statistics

SUMMARY

I. Descriptive Statistics: Telling It Like It Is
    A. **Frequency Distributions**
        1. are graphs that show how often scores of particular magnitudes appear in a group of scores
            a. Score values are plotted on the abscissa (or X axis)
            b. Frequencies are plotted on the ordinate (or Y axis)
        2. Examples of frequency distributions include the
            a. **Histogram** - or bar chart.
                (1) Vertical bars are drawn for each score value in the sample range, or for groups of score values.
                (2) The height of these bars is made to be proportional to the number of scores that fall in the range that the bar represents.
            b. **Frequency polygon** - a frequency distribution made by connecting the midpoints of the bars in a histogram.
    B. Measures of **Central Tendency**
        1. indicate the center of a distribution of scores, i.e. they indicate the most "typical" score in a group.
        2. Example of measures of central tendency
            a. the **mean** is
                (1) the most commonly used measure of central tendency
                (2) the arithmetic average of the scores in the sample
                (3) the measure most strongly influenced by extreme scores.

        b.   the **median** is
- (1) the middlemost score in a group; the number of scores exceeded by the median is the same as the number of scores that the median exceeds.
- (2) the median is often used when there are extreme scores in the sample.

        c.   the **mode** is
- (1) the value of the most frequent score
- (2) rarely reported in psychological research

C. Measures of Dispersion
1. indicate how much scores in a sample are spread out about the center
2. the **range** is
   - a. the simplest measure of dispersion
   - b. the difference between the highest and lowest scores in a sample
   - c. rarely used since it is based entirely on the extreme scores in a sample.
3. the **mean deviation** is
   - a. a useful measure of dispersion
   - b. the average absolute amount by which scores differ from the mean
   - c. rarely used
4. the **variance** is
   - a. the sum of the squared deviations from the mean, divided by the number of scores.
   - b. employed in inferential statistics
5. the **standard deviation** is
   - a. the square root of the variance
   - b. the most widely used measure of dispersion

II. The **Normal Distribution**
A. is a frequency distribution commonly found in psychological data.
B. In a normal distribution,
1. the mean, median, and mode all coincide
2. the scores are symmetrically distributed about the mean
3. the inflection points lie exactly one standard deviation from the mean
4. approximately 68% of the scores fall between -1 and +1 standard deviation from the mean, 96% between -2 and +2 standard deviations, and 99.74% between -3 and +3 standard deviations

C. **Standard scores**, or **z-scores**
1. indicate how many standard deviations individual scores lie above or below the mean.

2. *z*-scores are useful because they permit comparisons of measures of different characteristics.

KEY TERM MATCHING

1.

____ mean

____ mean deviation

____ median

____ mode

____ range

____ standard deviation

____ variance

____ *z*-score

a. arithmetic average
b. average absolute difference between scores and the group mean
c. difference between the highest and lowest scores
d. middlemost score
e. most commonly used measure of dispersion
f. number of standard deviations a particular score lies from the mean
g. sum of the squared deviations from the mean, divided by the number of scores
h. value of the most frequent score

2.

____ frequency distribution

____ frequency polygon

____ histogram

____ normal distribution

a. commonly observed shape of a frequency distribution for psychological data
b. constructed by connecting the midpoints of the bars in a bar graph
c. frequencies are indicated by the heights of vertical bars
d. general term for graphs that show how often particular score values occur in a sample

3.

____ measures of central tendency

____ measures of dispersion

____ inflection point

a. indicate how different the scores are from each other in a sample
b. lies one standard deviation from the median in a normal distribution
c. value of a most "typical" score in a sample

Programmed Review

1. The two main types of descriptive statistics are measures of _____ _____ and measures of _____.

2. One type of graphical representation of numerical data is a _____ or, bar graph.

3. The histogram and the _____ _____ are both examples of _____ distributions.

4. The most common measure of central tendency in psychological research is the _____.

5. The midpoint of the distribution is called the _____ while the most frequently occurring score in the distribution is called the _____.

6. A measure of central tendency that is relatively insensitive to extreme scores is the _____.

7. The difference between the highest and lowest scores in the distribution is called the _____.

8. When calculating the mean deviation, it is necessary to use the _____ value of the difference between each score and the group mean.

9. The _____ of a distribution is defined as the sum of the squared deviations from the mean divided by the number of scores.

10. The square root of the variance gives us the _____ _____ of the distribution.

11. The formula for the variance is $s^2 =$ _____

12. Psychologists typically present the _____ and the _____ _____ when describing a set of data.

13. A useful property of the normal curve is that a specific _____ of the scores fall under each part of the curve.

14. If two normal distributions have different means and variances then one way to compare scores across these two distributions is to convert the scores to _____ scores or _____ scores.

15. If we calculate the difference between an individual score and the mean of the distribution from which the score was taken, and then divide this difference by the standard deviation of the distribution, the resulting score represents a _____ score.

MULTIPLE CHOICE

1. Descriptive statistics
    a. summarize experimental observations.
    b. tell which data are important.
    c. indicate which differences are reliable.
    d. all of the above

2. The mean is:
    a. the same as the arithmetic average.
    b. the middle score.
    c. the most common score.
    d. the standard score.
    e. the extreme score.

3. The median is:
    a. the sum of scores divided by the number of scores.
    b. the most frequent score.
    c. the midpoint of the distribution of scores.
    d. the range of scores.

4. The primary reason the median is used is because
    a. it is the most useful measure of central tendency.
    b. it has the property of being insensitive to extreme scores.
    c. it has the property of accurately reflecting the range of scores.
    d. almost all inferential statistics are based on it.

5. The _____ is the most frequent score in a distribution.
    a. mode
    b. median
    c. mean
    d. range

6. What is the mode of this distribution?   1 3 4 4 6 9 11 12 15
    a. 4
    b. 6
    c. 7.2
    d. 14

7. The simplest measure of dispersion in a group of scores is the:
    a. mode.
    b. range.
    c. standard deviation.
    d. variance.
    e. *z*-score

8. A defining characteristic of the mean is that
    a. as n increases, the mean increases.
    b. the sum of the deviations of scores about the mean is always zero.
    c. the mean deviation equals the mean divided by *n*.
    d. the mean is always less than the range.

9. The variance of a distribution is defined as the _____ divided by the number of scores.
    a. sum of the absolute deviations from the mean
    b. differences between the highest and lowest scores
    c. sum of the squared deviations from the mean
    d. sum of the absolute deviations from the median

10. The square root of the variance is the
    a. standard deviation.
    b. average deviation.
    c. mean deviation.
    d. sample deviation.

11. In describing an array of data, psychologists typically present two descriptive statistics, which are
    a. the median and variance.
    b. the median and standard deviation.
    c. the mean and the variance.
    d. the mean and the standard deviation.

12. Which of the following is a characteristic of the standard normal distribution?
    a. The mean, median, and mode are the same.
    b. The mean and median only are the same.
    c. The median and mode only are the same.
    d. The mean and mode only are the same.
    e. none of the above

13. Approximately what percentage of scores in a normal distribution fall between plus and minus one standard deviation from the mean?
    a. 17%
    b. 34%
    c. 68%
    d. 96%
    e. 99.7%

14. Approximately what percentage of scores in a normal distribution have z-values between -2.0 and +2.0?
    a. 17%
    b. 34%
    c. 68%
    d. 96%
    e. 99.7%

TRUE-FALSE

____ 1. Another name for a histogram is a frequency polygon.

____ 2. The most common measure of central tendency in psychological research is the mean.

____ 3. Extremely small or large scores have an effect on the mean, but not on the mode or median.

____ 4. The mean of a set of scores has the property that the deviations from the mean add up to zero.

____ 5. The standard deviation is simply the square root of the variance.

____ 6. A property of the standard normal distribution is that the mean and the median are the same, but the mode is different.

____ 7. A z-score is the difference between an individual score and the mean expressed in units of standard deviation.

ANSWERS

KEY TERM MATCHING

1. a, b, d, h, c, e, g, f   2. d, b, c, a   3. c, a, b

PROGRAMMED REVIEW

1. Central tendency, dispersion; (p. 359)
2. histogram; (p. 360)
3. frequency polygon, frequency; (p. 360)
4. mean; (p. 360)
5. median, mode; (p. 360)
6. median; (p. 361)
7. range; (p. 362)
8. absolute; (p. 362)
9. variance; (p. 362)
10. standard deviation; (p. 362)
11. Variance=$(\Sigma(X\text{-Mean})^2)/n$
12. mean, standard deviation; (p. 365)
13. proportion; (p. 367)
14. standard, z; (p. 368)
15. z; (p. 367)

MULTIPLE CHOICE

1. a; (p. 359)	2. a; (p. 360)	3. c; (p. 361)
4. b; (p.361)	5. a; (p. 361)	6. a; (p. 361)
7. b; (p. 362)	8. b; (p. 362)	9. c; (p. 362)
10. a; (p. 362)	11. d; (p. 365)	12. a; (p. 366)
13. c; (p. 367)	14. d; (p. 367)	

TRUE-FALSE

1. F; (p. 359)	2. T; (p. 360)	3. T; (p. 361)
4. T; (p. 362)	5. T; (p. 362)	6. F; (p. 366)
7. T; (p. 366)		

APPENDIX B

Inferential Statistics

SUMMARY

I. Statistical Reasoning
    A. Inferential statistics helps us decide whether a difference between treatment means is due to chance or to the effect of our independent variable.
    B. Sampling
        1. A sample is a subset of the population to which we want to generalize our results
        2. Due to chance, different samples drawn from the population will have different means.
        3. The sample means of many samples drawn from the same population will be normally distributed: the mean of the sample means will be very close to the population mean.
        4. The variation (measured by the **standard error of the mean**) among the means of large samples drawn from a population is smaller than that of small samples. Hence, a single large sample is more likely to be representative of the population.
    C. Testing Hypotheses
        1. The experimenter generates a research hypothesis that an independent variable will produce some effect on a dependent variable.
        2. Data are collected, and some differences are found among the means of the treatment groups.
        3. Inferential statistics are used to determine the probability of obtaining differences as large as these, if the **null hypothesis** were true. The null hypothesis states that any differences found among treatment means is due to chance or sampling error.

4.   If the probability is smaller than **alpha** (a predetermined level of probability, often equal to .05) the null hypothesis is *rejected*, and **statistically reliable differences** are claimed.

5.   Two types of errors can occur in hypothesis testing:

    a.   a **type I error** is rejecting the null hypothesis then it is true. The frequency of this happening is a function of the alpha level.

    b.   a **type II error** is failing to reject the null hypothesis when it is false. The probability of a type II error can be reduced by increasing the size of the experimental groups.

6.   Hypothesis testing can be either directional or nondirectional

    a.   **Directional** research hypotheses predict the direction of the experimental effect. **One-tailed** statistical tests are used, which reduces the probability of type II errors, provided that the obtained difference is in the predicted direction. One tailed tests are used in applied research.

    b.   **Nondirectional** research hypotheses do not specify the direction of the effect of an independent variable. **Two-tailed** statistical tests are used, that are sensitive to differences in either direction. This more conservative approach is usually used in basic research.

II.   Statistical Tests

    A.   Tests for Differences Between Two Groups

        1.   Between-Subjects designs

            a.   The **Mann-Whitney *U* test** is used with ordinal level data.

            b.   The **between-subjects *t*-test** is used with interval level data.

        2.   Within-Subjects designs

            a.   The **Wilcoxon signed-ranks test** is used with ordinal level data.

            b.   The **within-subjects *t*-test** is used with interval level data

        3.   the **point-biserial** correlation (r_{pb}) can be used in conjunction with either *t*-test as a measure of the **magnitude of effect** of the independent variable.

    B.   The Analysis of Variance (ANOVA)

        1.   the ***F*-statistic** is a ratio of two independent estimates of the population variance.

            a.   The estimate in the numerator is based on differences among the means of the various groups in the experiment. This will be large if the independent variables affect behavior.

    b.   The estimate in the denominator is based on the spread of scores within each of the treatment groups. This should not be affected by the independent variable.

2.   According to the null hypothesis, the expected value of F is 1.0; if there are treatment effects, F will be larger than 1.0.

3.   The **one-way ANOVA** is used when there are more than two levels of a single independent variable, and a between-subject design is used.

4.   The within-subjects or **treatment X subjects ANOVA** is used for within-subjects designs involving a single independent variable.

5.   **Multifactor ANOVAs** are used for experiments with two or more independent variables.

KEY TERM MATCHING

1.

___ alpha level

___ directional test

___ nondirectional test

___ type-I error

___ type-II error

___ parameters

___ statistics

a. incorrectly rejecting the null hypothesis
b. inversely related to statistical power
c. measures of properties of populations
d. measures of properties of samples
e. probability criterion for statistical significance
f. research hypotheses predicts the direction of the effect of the independent variable
g. two-tailed test

2.

___ F-statistic

___ Mann-Whitney U test

___ multifactor ANOVA

___ one-way ANOVA

___ standard error of the mean

___ treatment X subject ANOVA

___ Wilcoxin signed-ranks test

a. between-subjects nonparametric test
b. decreases as the sample size increases
c. ratio of two estimated of the population variance
d. several levels of one independent variable, between-subjects
e. several levels of one independent variable, within-subjects
f. two or more independent variables
g. within-subject nonparametric test

PROGRAMMED REVIEW

1.   A complete set of measurements (or individual or objects) having some common observable characteristic is called a _____ .

2.   A subset of a population is called a _____ .

3.   If we conducted an experiment and then replicated that same experiment many times, the distribution of the resultant sample means would tend to be a _____ distribution.

4.   The standard deviation of a distribution of sample means is called the _____ of the _____ .

5.   In general we want the standard error of the mean to be as _____ as possible. One way to do this is to _____ the size of the sample.

6.   In testing hypotheses we pit the _____ hypothesis against the _____ hypothesis.

7.   The null hypothesis predicts that

_____

_____

8.   If we know the standard deviation of the population then we can find the standard error of the mean by dividing the population standard deviation by_____

_____

9.   If you are told that an observed difference was significant at the .05 level of confidence then this means that

_____

_____

10.   Rejecting the null hypothesis when it is actually true is called a Type _____ error, and the probability that this error is being made is indexed by the _____ level.

11.   If we fail to reject the null hypothesis when it is in fact false, then we have committed a Type _____ error.

12.   A conservative statistical test minimizes Type _____ errors.

13.   The _____ of a test is the probability of rejecting the null hypothesis

when it is actually false.

14. By increasing the _____ _____ we may increase the power of our test.

15. If the alternative hypothesis specifies the direction of the expected difference, then a _____-tailed test is used, but if the alternative hypothesis is nondirectional then a _____-tailed test is used.

16. Two-tailed tests are more _____ and _____ powerful than one-tailed tests.

17. A _____ statistical test is one that makes assumptions about the underlying population parameters of the samples on which the tests are performed.

18. In general _____ tests are less powerful than _____ tests employed in the same situation.

19. The Mann-Whitney U test is used to analyze data from a _____-subject design. The Wilcoxin signed-ranks test is used to analyze data from a _____-_____ design.

20. If a researcher used four levels of an independent variable and tested four separate groups of subjects, an appropriate statistical test for analyzing the data from this experiment would be a simple _____ _____ _____.

21. The F-test used in the analysis of variance is a ratio of the _____-groups variance estimate to the _____-groups variance estimate.

22. The null hypothesis predicts that the F-ratio should be _____.

23. In an experiment in which more than one factor is varied simultaneously the appropriate procedure for analyzing the results would be to use a _____ analysis of variance.

MULTIPLE CHOICE

1. Inferential statistics are concerned with
   a. the importance of data.
   b. the meaning of data.
   c. the reliability of data.
   d. all of the above

2. Characteristics of a population of scores are called _____, while characteristics of a sample of scores drawn from a larger population are _____.
   a. statistics; parameters
   b. parameters; statistics
   c. generalizations; data
   d. inferences; facts

3. The distribution of sample means tends to be
   a. normal.
   b. exponential.
   c. Poisson.
   d. random.

4. The standard error of the mean is the
   a. square root of the mean.
   b. mean of a distribution of sample means
   c. variance of a distribution of sample means
   d. standard deviation of a distribution of sample means

5. The standard error of the mean represents the error we have in assuming that
   a. the mean represents the sample mean.
   b. the sample mean represents the population mean.
   c. the standard deviation of the sample mean is accurate.
   d. the standard deviation of the population mean is accurate.

6. As the sample size (n) increases,
   a. the sample mean increases.
   b. the standard error of the mean increases.
   c. the standard error of the mean decreases.
   d. the standard deviation of the mean increases.

7. The null hypothesis suggests that
   a. the two samples come from the same distribution.
   b. the two samples come from different distributions.
   c. the two samples come from different but overlapping. distributions.
   d. the two samples come from different but similar distributions

8. Adopting a .05 level of confidence means that you would
   a. accept the null hypothesis if the results could occur 5 times in 100 by chance.
   b. reject the null hypothesis if the results could occur 5 times in 100 by chance.
   c. reject the experimental hypothesis if the results could occur 5 times in 100 by chance.
   d. none of the above

9. An experimental psychologist reports that his statistical test indicates that the difference between his experimental and control group in his latest experiment is highly significant. By this he means that
   a. the difference was highly unlikely to have occurred by chance.
   b. the difference was probably due to chance factors.
   c. the results are very important.
   d. both a and c

10. Rejecting the null hypothesis when it is actually true is
    a. a Type I error.
    b. a Type II error.
    c. a Type III error.
    d. a standard error.
    e. not an error; it's the right thing to do.

11. A Type I error occurs when you:
    a. reject a false null hypothesis.
    b. reject a true null hypothesis.
    c. reject a true experimental hypothesis.
    d. accept a false null hypothesis.

12. In hypothesis testing, both magnitude of the difference and the direction of the difference between two groups are considered in
    a. two-tailed tests.
    b. one-tailed tests.
    c. parametric tests.
    d. nonparametric tests.

13. Parametric tests
    a. do not make assumptions about the underlying population parameters.
    b. make assumptions about the underlying population parameters.
    c. are typically more powerful than nonparametric tests.
    d. both b and c

14. Mann-Whitney U-test can only be used for
    a.   within-subjects designs.
    b.   between-subjects designs.
    c.   repeated measures designs.
    d.   none of the above

True False

___ 1.   A population is a complete set of measurements (or individuals or objects) having some common observable characteristics.

___ 2.   The distribution of sample means is not a normal distribution.

___ 3.   As the sample size (n) increases, the standard error of the mean decreases, the power of the statistical test increases, and the probability of a Type II error decreases.

___ 4.   The null hypothesis maintains that the two samples of scores (experimental and control) come from two different underlying distributions.

___ 5.   Adopting a .05 level of confidence means that you would accept the null hypothesis if the obtained difference could occur 5 times in 100 by chance.

___ 6.   A Type I error is rejecting the null hypothesis when it is actually true.

___ 7.   A liberal statistical test minimizes the probability of making a Type II error.

___ 8.   One way to increase the power of a statistical test is to increase the sample size.

___ 9.   A two-tailed statistical test considers both the magnitude of the difference and the direction of the differences between two groups.

___ 10.   Nonparametric tests are those that make assumptions about the underlying population parameters while parametric tests do not make such assumptions.

____ 11.   A simple analysis of variance (ANOVA) uses only one dependent variable whereas a complex or multifactor ANOVA uses more than one dependent variable.

____ 12.   In an analysis of variance, the F-ratio under the null hypothesis should equal 0.00.

ANSWERS

KEY TERM MATCHING

1. e, f, g, a, b, c, d   2. b, a, f, j, i, h, e, f, g, c, d

PROGRAMMED REVIEW

1.   population; (p. 373)
2.   sample; (p. 374)
3.   normal; (p. 375)
4.   standard error, mean; (p. 376)
5.   small, increase; (p. 377)
6.   null, experimental; (p. 378)
7.   the experimental and control scores come from the same population; (p. 378)
8.   the square root of one less than the sample size; (p. 377)
9.   the probability of obtaining a difference as large as this by chance is less than 5 in 100; (p. 379)
10.   type I error, alpha; (p. 379)
11.   II;; (p. 381)
12.   I; (p. 381)
13.   power; (p. 382)
14.   sample size; (p. 382)
15.   one, two;; (p. 383)
16.   conservative, powerful; (p. 384)
17.   parametric; (p. 384)
18.   nonparametric, parametric;; (p. 385)
19.   between, within-subject; (p. 385)
20.   analysis of variance; (p. 394)

21. between, within; (p. 394)
22. 1.0; (p. 395)
23. multifactor; (p. 401)

MULTIPLE CHOICE

1. c; (p. 373)   2. b; (p. 374)   3. a; (p. 375)

4. d; (p. 376)   5. b; (p. 377)   6. c; (p. 377)

7. a; (p. 378)   8. b; (p. 379)   9. a; (p. 380)

10. a; (p. 381)   11. b; (p. 381)   12. a; (p. 383)

13. d; (p. 384)   14. b; (p. 385)

True False

1. T; (p. 373)   2. F; (p. 375)   3. T; (p. 377)

4. F; (p. 378)   5. F; (p. 379)   6. T; (p. 381)

7. T; (p. 381)   8. T; (p. 382)   9. T; (p. 383)

10. F; (p. 384)   11. F; (p. 401)   12. F; (p. 395)